With.
Daring
Faith

A Biography of Amy Carmichael

by Rebecca Henry Davis

12/25/88
Katie —
I want to read this too!
Mom ♡

Bob Jones University Press, Greenville, South Carolina 29614

With Daring Faith

Edited by Suzette Jordan

Cover and illustrations by Stephanie True

©1987 by Bob Jones University Press
Greenville, South Carolina 29614

ISBN 0-89084-414-3
Printed in the United States of America

20 19 18 17 16 15 14 13 12 11 10 9 8 7

To Katherine Joy Davis
with the prayer that she will hear and
answer a call from the Lord
to a foreign mission field

Publisher's Note

In 1903 Amy Carmichael's book *Things as They Are* shocked many complacent Englishmen and Americans into looking more closely at conditions in India. It was the first of many books about Amy Carmichael's work in India, and it has been followed by others from Amy Carmichael herself as well as from writers who carefully followed her ministry. Surprisingly, there has never yet been a complete children's biographical novel of Miss Carmichael's life published in the United States. Although publishers have made short stories and other materials about her work available for young people, *With Daring Faith* is the first children's book to cover the entire life of Amy Carmichael.

Absolutely fearless of man's opinion, Amy Carmichael was given grace in her life to follow the dictates of her Lord without holding back. She was one of the first missionaries in India to adopt Indian dress, and amid both missionaries and Indian Christians who considered manual labor dishonorable, she cheerfully settled down to doing her share of the work with the Dohnavur children.

Her close relationship with the Lord led her to a clear and consistent course of action throughout events that could have been occasions for stumbling. Her careful treatment of divine healing, for instance, serves as a positive example for the modern reader, who finds himself today with the un-Biblical example of the charismatic movement.

But the qualities of Amy Carmichael that stand out today—even as they stood out during her life at Dohnavur—are her daring faith, her overcoming spirit, and her tender love for the children she sought to rescue. The love that the Lord gave her for children led her into a kind of double life. Even she recognized that she was able to spend a morning in agonizing prayer, weeping for the children already doomed to the temples, and yet emerge in the afternoon to cuddle and play with the Dohnavur children, weaving a web of love and happiness around them.

The secret to her unwavering love for her children was her unwavering love for the Lord. This love led her to the place of prayer, and she wrote in advice to other missionaries that—important as it was to be up and about at work—the Christian servant's most important place of service is the place of prayer. Amy Carmichael was a part of the Lord's army in India, and the battles that she won were first won on her knees. She refused to go out to the warfare until she knew exactly what it was that the Lord wanted her to do for Him.

We hope that *With Daring Faith* will be a first step for our readers in discovering the wealth of insight and challenge that missionary biographies can offer. No single biography, no matter how exhaustive, can completely capture the image of a person's soul. In addition to this book, there are many others, written by Amy Carmichael herself, that describe what the Lord did in India to break the chains of darkness on His people there. We hope that our readers will be awakened to the treasures that lie in the writings of great Christian servants.

Contents

Chapter One

Brown Eyes, Blue Eyes

Yes, they were brown. Brown, brown, brown. As brown as two dirty mud puddles. She opened her eyes wide to stare at them in the mirror again. But staring didn't make them any bluer.

Amy climbed down from the chair and pushed it to the nursery window. The sea there on the coast of Ireland was as blue as the sky today, just the way she liked it best. When it was gray or green, some people liked it. But only the blue for her. It was the most beautiful color in the world. Amy went into the kitchen and pulled on her mother's skirt.

"Yes, Amy?" Mama slid the chicken into the oven, pushed a wisp of light brown hair away from her face, and knelt down for her daughter. Her blue eyes, still beautiful even though they looked tired, made Amy bite her lip with envy.

"Mama . . ." she began. Then she hesitated while she thought of the best way to put her question. She knew from experience that Mama sometimes explained things even when Amy just wanted a simple

1

yes or no answer. "Mama, doesn't Jesus answer prayer?"

"Yes, He certainly does, Amy, darling. He will always answer prayer if it is prayed from a sincere and loving heart."

"I know it, Mama, and I love you, and I love your blue eyes. They make you just right."

Her mother laughed and hugged Amy. "My blue eyes don't make me any better, Amy. And besides, you have beautiful eyes too. Such a lovely brown."

But Amy couldn't be convinced that brown eyes were lovely. That night her mother prayed with her as usual and turned the nursery light down low. When Amy was alone, she invited Jesus to come sit by her on the bed, just as she always did. But this time she prayed, "Dear Lord Jesus, please make my eyes blue. I love You. Amen. Good night." And she fell asleep, never doubting for a moment that when she awoke her eyes would be just as beautiful as Mama's.

When Amy awoke in the morning, her heart beat hard with hope and excitement. She tumbled out of bed and pushed the chair back to the dresser to gaze at her beautiful blue eyes in the mirror. She climbed up and looked. Her eyes were still brown.

"Mama!" she wailed. She ran into the kitchen where her mother was mixing the dough for breakfast biscuits. "Mama, you said that if I prayed I could get blue eyes!"

Mama burst out laughing. "Amy, lamb, I never said any such thing. Are you talking about what I said yesterday about the Lord Jesus answering prayer?"

Speechless with disappointment, Amy nodded. Mama pressed the dough flat and cut out three biscuits before she spoke again. "Amy, sometimes when you want something very badly, Papa and I know it's not best for you. And we have to tell you no. But you know that we do it because we love you, don't you?"

Amy eyed her mother doubtfully, sensing another explanation that she wouldn't really like as much as a simple yes or no. "But you said that Jesus would always give me what I wanted if I loved Him. And I do love Him."

"No, darling, I didn't say He would give you what you wanted. I said He would *answer* you. And when you asked for blue eyes, He said no. Isn't *no* an answer?"

"But why wouldn't He give me blue eyes when anybody can see that they're better than brown ones?"

Mama rolled the dough out again and cut out five more biscuits. The last one she shaped into a heart. "Amy, remember one thing. Jesus loves you very, very much. Since He gave you brown eyes, you can be sure that brown eyes were right for you. We don't know why. But they were. And when you prayed last night, Jesus said, 'Amy, I know that you love Me. But I can't give you what you ask for because it isn't best. I have to say no.'" Mama slid the pan of biscuits into the oven.

Amy climbed up into her chair for breakfast, pondering this new thought. Although she was only three, she knew perfectly well that Jesus loved her. But she had never realized that perhaps Jesus didn't always say yes to everything a child of His asked for. Mama popped the hot biscuits onto a plate and smiled as she handed Amy the heart-shaped one. The breakfast smelled good, and she was hungry, but she sighed as she took a bite. There were a lot of things about Jesus that she didn't understand. But He loved her. She knew that for sure.

Chapter Two
The Mouse and the Governess

"Just one more stitch here and I'll be ready to start the *6 ,*" Amy murmured, half to herself. "Mother, I'm glad I'm grown-up enough to be making a sampler, but it does get awfully dull sometimes."

"But someday you'll be so happy to have it, Amy girl." Mother smiled as she looked up from her mending. "Just think, someday you'll hold up this sampler to your husband and say, 'This was the first sampler I ever made, just after I turned eight years old.' And it will show the year there, and your verse."

"Yes." Amy giggled. " 'Rejoice evermore,' because it was one of the shortest verses I could find. But *1876* takes just as long to stitch as any other year. Really, Mother, how can we rejoice evermore? Does that mean we're supposed to sing all the time? It seems that it would really get in the way of trying to carry on a conversation or sleep or eat or even pray. Is there some other kind of rejoicing?"

"I just don't know how your father wears holes in his socks so quickly. It seems that I have to darn another pair every other day." Mother bit the yarn and knotted it before she stopped to think. Then she laughed a little. "I just gave a good example of *not* rejoicing. Rejoicing is more than just singing or even praying. Rejoicing is being thankful for everything you have all the time."

"Even the bad things and the hard things?"

"Yes, even those. Amy, I hear Ethel crying. You may go outside and play with your little brothers for a while before family worship. But make sure you bundle up. You always seem to be getting sick this time of year."

"Thank you, Mother. I will!" Amy had been longing to go outside and enjoy the sunshine since the day had promised to be blue, but she'd had to work on her sampler first. As she quickly put away her sewing and ran to get her coat and scarf, she heard Mother's sweet voice singing to Ethel.

> When I survey the wondrous cross,
> On which the Prince of glory died,
> My richest gain I count but loss,
> And pour contempt on all my pride.

Even as she was trying to hurry, Amy felt that voice make a funny feeling in her heart. "I wish I could sing as sweetly as Mother does," she thought as she tugged on a boot. She remembered that it had been because of that song four years ago that she had first heard the story of Jesus' death on the cross. It had stunned her to think that one so dear and good could be killed like that. But Mother had helped her see that it was for her, for Amy, that He had let Himself be killed. Now she stopped and softly sang the next verse with Mother's voice before running outside.

See, from His head, His hands, His feet,
Sorrow and love flow mingled down;
Did e'er such love and sorrow meet,
Or thorns compose so rich a crown?

She felt a little solemn as she ran outside. But then Ernest called, "It's Amy! Now we're going to have some fun!" And Alfred echoed, "Yea, Amy!"

Amy struggled through the soft snow to reach the fort that her brothers were building. She enjoyed her reputation as Chief Fun-Lover and Mischief-Maker of the family. By the time they heard Mother ringing the bell for family worship, the three children had bright red noses and damp hair from all the snowballs they had thrown at each other.

Stomping up the steps they came, one after another, shaking the snow off their scarves and sleeves, teeth chattering. Suddenly Amy stopped and knelt in front of the pail of water beside the door.

"What's the matter, Amy?" Ernest asked.

"Shh!" Amy beckoned them out of her way. "It's a little mouse. He probably climbed up for a drink, and then he broke through the ice and fell in. We have to rescue him."

"Looks like he's dead to me," Alfred said dubiously.

"Besides, what're you going to do?" Ernest demanded. "We have to go in for family worship *right now.*"

Amy's brown eyes sparkled. "Yes, I'm coming. You two go on in. I'll be right there."

The two little brothers might not have obeyed except that they heard their father's deep voice calling each name in turn, and they knew that if they didn't go immediately, they could be spanked.

"Come *on,* Amy!" Ernest urged.

"I'm coming! I'll be right there! But don't tell anyone we saw this mouse." And Amy watched as her two little brothers trooped into the house.

When she ran in a few moments later, cheeks flushed and eyes bright, she saw everyone gathered in a circle in the sitting room. All Father said was, "We're glad you could come tonight, Amy." Ernest and Alfred giggled.

"I'm sorry I'm late, Father," Amy murmured, and she slid into her place. Father began to read.

"Make a joyful noise unto the Lord, all the earth: make a loud noise, and rejoice, and sing praise. Sing unto the Lord with the harp; with the harp, and the voice of a psalm. With trumpets and sound of cornet make a joyful noise before the Lord, the King.

"Let the sea roar, and the fulness thereof; the world, and they that dwell therein. Let the floods clap their hands: let the hills be joyful together."

Amy leaned forward, imagining the sound of the sea roaring, the blue sea, the gray sea, the green sea, roaring the majesty of God. She imagined the floods clapping their hands in praise of Him. What beautiful verses! What wonderful things to ima—

Suddenly she started and put a hand over one pocket, which was wiggling. She glanced around the room, but no one had seemed to notice. Once more she relaxed.

"Let us be sure to pray for Reverend Beatty," Father was saying. "His legs are becoming so crippled that he is concerned about having a way to visit the members of his congregation. Did you say something, Amy?"

Amy blushed scarlet, for a muffled squeak had just issued from the pocket of her pinafore. "No, Father," she whispered. Ernest's eyes got big, and he began to bounce up and down on the chair. Amy shot daggers at him with her eyes. Another squeak, this time louder, wrestled its way through the choking fabric.

"Amy, what is it?" Father asked. He looked out at her from under his heavy eyebrows.

Miserably, Amy pulled the struggling little mouse from her pocket, being careful to hold it by the neck so that it wouldn't bite her. "Oh!" Mother almost jumped from her chair. She held Ethel a little closer.

Father covered his mouth with his hand and looked stern. "And why, Amy, have you believed it necessary to bring a mouse in to participate in family worship?" Ernest and Alfred both stifled a laugh.

"I didn't, Father," Amy gasped. "I mean, I didn't think the mouse could participate in family worship. I may have thought once that a mouse should hear about Jesus, but I don't anymore. It was just that this poor little mouse was about to drown in the bucket of water outside, and if I took him out and left him outside, he would have frozen to death, all wet like that, but if I put him in my pocket and held him close to me for just a few minutes, he would feel better, and now you can see that he really does—why, I think he's ready to go right back outside and return to his family, don't you?" She stopped to take another breath, and cast pleading eyes upon her father, pleading more for her own well-being than for that of the mouse.

"I think it is far better if you take him outside at once," Father agreed. "And we will talk more about this later." Amy could see that Ernest and Alfred wanted to burst with laughter but held it in, since this was family worship time. She trudged miserably to the door, figuring that she would probably get a spanking for bringing the mouse inside.

"Amy, I don't know how you could have done such a thing," Mother said the next day. "Especially when we have a baby in the house. Why, that mouse could have gotten loose and bitten Ethel."

"I'm sorry, Mother." Amy sighed deeply. "It's just that when I see an animal in trouble I don't even stop to think about things like that. I just want to help it. I couldn't stand to think of that poor little mouse drowning or freezing to death."

"Well, I don't know what we'll do with you. You seem to care too much about things that aren't very important." She paused. "I do have two secrets to tell you, though."

"Oh, Mother, tell me! I just love secrets! Are they secrets just for me? Or are they secrets that you're going to tell everybody else, too—"

Mother laughed. "Just calm down with your figuring. They're secrets for you to know now and the others to know later. One is that Father and I have felt called on from the Lord to give the Reverend Beatty a horse and carriage so that he can visit the members of his congregation."

Amy sucked in her breath and wrapped her arms around herself. "How wonderful! I mean, it's so good and noble of you and Father, and now Reverend Beatty will be able to visit everyone, and he'll owe it all to you. I'm sure the Lord will bless you for it. That's what they always say—that when you give, the Lord will give back to you ever so much more than you gave in the first place. That's what they say."

"Fiddlesticks, Amy. We didn't do it to be noble, and we didn't do it to be blessed. We did it because we saw a need, and we had the means to provide it. Yes, the Lord will bless us, but it won't necessarily be by giving us a finer carriage or a better horse. It may be—it probably *will* be—in the comfort and assurance of seeing our beloved pastor once again able to do what the Lord has called him to do. And that is enough for us. It should always be enough for anyone who gives to the Lord. Don't you ever forget that."

"Yes, Mother—I mean, no, Mother—I won't." Amy's eyes shone like stars, though her voice was considerably subdued. "Now tell me the other secret, if you please."

"The other secret is that next week you and the boys will be getting a governess."

"A *governess?* Mother, what do we need with a governess? We're perfectly good as we are!"

"It isn't that you aren't perfectly good—though I'll warrant that even that idea could be contested—it's that you need some schooling, and a governess can provide what your father and I cannot."

"But what will she be like? Will she be big and fat and ugly?"

"Why, no, as a matter of fact; though indeed, big, fat, ugly ladies can be just as nice as slender, pretty ones. She is young and well groomed, and she seems as if she'll order things quite nicely. I don't think she'll take any funny business."

Amy plopped down into a chair, distraught. "I was afraid of that," she groaned.

Indeed, the new governess, Miss O'Shea, turned out to be true to Mrs. Carmichael's word. She never smiled or seemed to be able to take a joke; she spoke in an annoying nasal voice and sniffed at the antics and games of the children. She made life so miserable for Amy, Ernest, and Alfred that by springtime they decided to make life miserable for her in turn. They had no trouble in catching frogs and bugs, little creatures that they had often caught just for fun anyway. More than once Miss O'Shea lifted a cup of tea to her lips only to find an earwig in it, swimming desperately for his life, or to climb into bed only to find that she had to oust a disgruntled toad in the process. After a few weeks of such treatment, the governess announced to Mrs. Carmichael that she was packing her bags.

Both Mr. and Mrs. Carmichael were distressed to find that things had come to such a turn, but the governess could not be dissuaded. Amy watched out the window to see when Miss O'Shea's ride came. Then she ran to her brothers' room. "Come on!" she whispered urgently. "Let's go down and see her off!"

Ernest looked at her doubtfully. "Why do you want to do that, Amy?" he asked. "Do you think we should to tell her we're sorry?"

"Oh, no!" Amy answered with a snort. "I just want to watch her and make sure she really goes."

But when the three trooped downstairs, they faced two angry parents. Father took the two boys into one room, and Mother took Amy into her own bedroom. "Amy," Mother began, "you, as the oldest, are the most responsible for the dreadful misconduct that resulted in Miss O'Shea's leaving so quickly. I am sorely grieved with you."

"Yes, Mother," Amy answered sullenly. She looked down and traced a pattern on the floor with the tip of her shoe.

"And to think that Uncle William tells his five children that they should all be as good as you and your brothers."

"But I never asked him to say that."

"If Miss O'Shea was too hard on you, you could have brought your complaint to us and had it dealt with properly. What you did was wrong."

"She deserved every bit of it, Mother. Every bit! She never even tried to make us like her. She was horrible—"

"Amy Beatrice Carmichael!" Mother took in her breath. "You should never talk about anyone that way."

Amy still didn't cringe, even though Mother had used her full name. She felt the most defiant and willful she had felt in a long time, and she folded her arms together to prove it.

For a few seconds mother and daughter stood gazing at each other. Finally Mother said, "Child, sit there on that green stool. I am going out now." And she took up her bonnet from the dresser and stood in front of the mirror tying the strings slowly and deliberately. Amy looked up in spite of herself and saw her mother's reflection in the mirror. Such a grieved look she had never seen before, and even as she watched, tears trickled down Mother's cheek, tears of grief for a daughter who would not repent of the wrong she had done.

Suddenly Amy's hard heart seemed to tear inside of her, and she ran to her mother and threw her arms around her, as tears came to her own eyes. "Oh, Mother, I don't know why sometimes I let Satan take over and do whatever he wants to with me. I don't know why I don't please Jesus all the time. I want to. Truly I do. Now, anyway. I didn't before, but I do now." Her words were cut off by a catch in her throat. Then she added, "Please forgive me."

Mother turned around and took her little girl in her arms. Punishment might have to come later, but all was forgiven.

Chapter Three
More Adventures

After Miss O'Shea left the Carmichael household, several other governesses came and went, all leaving for one reason or another, some to get married, some to go home to sick parents, but never again did one leave for the same reason Miss O'Shea did.

Finally, the Carmichaels found a governess who was exactly suited to everyone's needs, and they to hers. Eleanor Milne taught the Carmichael children not only their school subjects but also love and care for all God's creatures, and she told them wonderful stories of great Christian martyrs.

Sometimes Amy, now ten, told Eleanor stories of the many adventures and misadventures she'd had. Often Eleanor would laugh so hard she would have to reach for a handkerchief to wipe her eyes.

Amy told of the time that she persuaded her two little brothers to stand on the sea wall with her so that the spray could drench them thoroughly. My, how wonderful it was to feel the mighty ocean spray! They gave not a thought to the punishment they would receive when they got home with soaking wet clothes.

"Another time—" Amy clasped her knees and grinned as Eleanor shook with laughter—"another time, when our parents were out, Ernest and Alfred and I decided to climb through the skylight in the bathroom so that we could walk on the roof. I'd been longing to walk on the roof ever since I'd realized I could get there through the skylight. I'm not sure how we managed to get up there and get through it, but we did, and there we were! I slid down the roof so that I could walk around the gutter, and of course Ernest and Alfred followed me. And who do you think we should see as soon as we got to the edge? It was Mother and Father, back from their errand, staring up at us! They made us crawl back down through the bathroom skylight, and they stood in there, waiting to catch us as we came down. I'm not too eager to tell you what happened next."

But Eleanor's favorite story was of the time that Amy and her two younger brothers were outside swinging on the gate one day. Amy looked out and saw a laburnum tree near the road. "Laburnum pods are supposed to be poisonous," she said to her little brothers. "Let's count how many we can eat before we die." For Ernest and Alfred, Amy's word was as good as a command, so they all three ran to the tree and started gobbling down laburnum pods for all they were worth. Before long, all three of them were feeling sick to their stomachs. They all stood around the tree and held their stomachs, moaning for all they were worth, laburnum pods forgotten. It was this way that Mother found them not much later.

When they explained their tale of woe to her, she said simply, "It will be Gregory for you, children."

"Oh, no, Mother, not Gregory!" they all protested at once. "Not Gregory, please! We promise that we'll never do it again."

"It doesn't matter what you promise. You'll be sick if you don't take it. Come inside." And behind the kind but forceful woman trooped three sad little children.

Once inside, Mother prepared a tray holding a jug of water, a jug of milk, a tea cup, a spoon, and a bottle of Gregory, the awful-tasting pink powder that was designed to be a remedy for stomach ailments, but ended up being a terrible punishment for wrongdoing as well. As she stirred up the Gregory in the cup of milk, each child in turn had to say "Thank you, Mother" and drain the cup to the last drop.

All three of them got well after only a few minutes. Whether or not it was because of Gregory, Amy really couldn't say, but she did assure Eleanor that none of them ever again ate laburnum pods!

Eleanor tried to help the Carmichael children stay out of trouble. But a couple of years later, when Amy was about twelve, she and her brothers came the closest yet to losing their lives. The current along the coast of Strangford Lough was among the strongest currents in the world, and she and Ernest and Alfred could row their boat only within certain limits. But one evening the three of them carelessly went past the limits and found that they could no longer guide the little boat back to shore. The fierce current started pulling them closer and closer to a sandbar out in the water, where the boat would surely be damaged and sink.

"What should we do?" Alfred yelled wildly.

"Row! Row with all your might!" Amy screamed back.

Ernest and Alfred struggled with their oars. "It's not helping," Ernest said. "We can't do it. We're not strong enough."

"Why didn't we pay attention to where the boat was going? Row!" And while Amy tried to work the rudder, the two boys tried to row again with new vigor, but to no avail.

"Amy!" Ernest yelled suddenly. "Sing! Sing for all you're worth!"

Wildly, the wind whipping her hair, still struggling with the rudder, Amy yelled out the first song that came to her mind.

> He leadeth me, O blessed thought!
> O words with heavenly comfort fraught!
> What-e'er I do, where-e'er I be,
> Still 'tis God's hand that leadeth me.

"Sing it again! Sing another verse!"

"You sing with me this time!"

So all three sang fervently, struggling all the time with the oars that seemed powerless against the terrible power of the current.

"Look!" Amy called hoarsely. "Look! Isn't that the coastguard?"

"Yes, it is! We're saved! We're saved!"

Indeed it was the coastguard, come to their rescue upon hearing the song sung so frantically. Amy had to admit that God's hand had probably not led her and her brothers out past their limits, but she did rejoice that His hand had led the coastguard to rescue them.

The three bedraggled children knew that they would be in for punishment again when Father heard of how they had disobeyed his strict orders, even though they hadn't meant to. But when they got home, they found that Reverend Beatty was visiting, with some other people they had never seen before; so punishment was postponed. After they had changed their clothes, the three children came back to the parlor to meet the visitors.

"Amy, Ernest, Alfred, this is my brother and his wife, Mr. and Mrs. Beatty," Reverend Beatty said. "We all rode over here in that beautiful carriage that your father and mother gave us. My brother and sister-in-law are missionaries to India, home for a year of rest. They will be living in the house next door."

Amy came to love Mrs. Beatty, who would gather several children on Sunday afternoons and tell them stories of India. Even after all the other children had left, Amy still wanted to hear more. She loved to listen to the stories of how the Lord worked in the hearts of the Indian people who had never heard about Him. Of course, Amy had not yet been saved, and so she didn't know how the Lord was planning to use her in that vast country, but He was already at work, preparing her mind and attitude for His service.

Chapter Four
Boarding School

Amy loved her life in Millisle. Her many adventures served only to make it more enjoyable and exciting. As Ethel and then a new little sister, Eva, grew older, she included them in the fun too. When two more little brothers were born, she helped take care of them. Even though Amy herself was often in poor health, she still liked to go with her mother to take soup to the old and the poor.

But the day came when Amy's parents decided to send her to boarding school so that she could have more education.

When this news came, Amy wasn't the only one to moan. Ernest had to leave for a boy's school about the same time. The younger ones cried at the thought of losing their brother and their beloved sister. Amy sometimes got into fights with them but always made up for it with her tender heart and her fun-loving ways.

But Amy packed her bags and headed for Yorkshire, to the Marlborough House school for young ladies. The year was 1880, and she was thirteen.

Amy arrived, luggage in hand, to peer at a severe-looking woman behind a desk. The woman eyed this skinny, plain girl with the two brown braids stuck out behind her.

"And what might be your name, child?"

"Beatrice Carmichael, ma'am."

"I see here on this paper that your full name is Amy Beatrice Carmichael. Perhaps we should call you Amy."

Amy wanted to ask why the woman had asked her name if she already knew it. But instead she said, "Please, ma'am, don't call me Amy. It's such a silly little name, and I feel so grown-up being away from home here at school and all, even though I am a little frightened and shy, I must admit. But Beatrice is a lovely, adult name, and I think I could live with that. I just can't bear the name Amy any more."

"Very well, Beatrice. The house mistress here will show you to your room. Classes begin promptly at seven in the morning."

Amy met some friendly girls in her room and in the rooms nearby. But most of them eyed her as a creature from the wild, as indeed she almost was. Millisle was a strange and faraway place to girls who had been raised in the city.

But it didn't take Amy long to make friends with many of the girls there, regardless of whether they were from the city. Her kindness and gentleness with the smaller girls won her instant favor with them. And the older girls soon learned that Beatrice Carmichael had more than one trick up her sleeve. She could think up some of the best ways to have fun! And the rules, which were strict, proved a challenge to an unruly Irish country girl who didn't seem to mind being punished over and over.

"Beatrice!" whispered a new girl one night when they were supposed to be studying in the study room. "I heard one of the mistresses call you *Amy* today. Is that really your name?"

"Yes, but it's a great trial to me. I just don't care for it at all. It was fine for me when I was a child, but now I need to have an adult name, and *Beatrice* works fine."

"But I think *Amy* is beautiful. What does it mean?"

"Well, it means 'beloved,' " Amy answered somewhat grudgingly. "At least, that's what my mother told me."

"Beloved! That's just beautiful! I don't see why you don't want to be called by that name."

"Well, you can call me that if you really want to, I guess."

Some months later, when Amy heard that the Great Comet of 1882 was going to pass overhead one night, she and several other girls got together, determined to think of a way to see it.

"Come now, Amy," her new friend coaxed, "let's just ask Miss Kay if we can stay up and see it."

"Yes, Beatrice," chimed in another girl. "And you'd be the perfect one. We know that Miss Kay really likes you."

"Yes," Amy answered wryly, "she gives me whippings so often that she's become quite attached to me."

"Oh, please ask her, please do," the girls begged.

So Amy Beatrice Carmichael strode with determination right up to Miss Kay. She said in her most polite tones, "Miss Kay, may some of the older girls be allowed to stay up and see the Great Comet as it passes overhead tonight?"

"Certainly not," said Miss Kay.

"But Miss Kay," Amy blurted out, "it would be a tremendously beneficial scientific experience. I'm sure we would learn from it. And we would go straight to bed after we've seen it, and then we could tell the younger girls about it in the morning—or—or not mention even a word of it, if that would please you. And then in later years we could tell about it to our grandchildren, and they would be forever grateful to you, Miss Kay, for letting us stay up and see the Great Comet which we would describe to them in such vivid detail."

"Certainly not," said Miss Kay.

"But, Miss Kay—"

"No, Beatrice. Return to your studies."

So Amy returned, to announce the miserable failure of her attempt to her friends. But while they all sat bemoaning their fate, Amy had a sudden idea.

"Well, it *is* coming in the middle of the night, you know," she began. All the girls leaned closer. "And everyone else will be asleep; so if just we climbed up to the attic to see the comet out the window, no one would ever need to know about it, and then we would come right back to bed, and we would have that wonderful memory to carry all through our lives."

"But, Amy, how in the world would we ever stay up until that time of night?" her friend objected. "There's no way we could."

"Unless . . . unless only *one* of us had to stay awake. I know! I'll tie a string around the big toe of every one of you. And I'll stay awake until I'm sure that everyone else in the house is asleep, and then I'll pull all the strings at once, and we can sneak up to the attic!"

"It sounds terrible!" giggled one girl.

"Terribly exciting!" agreed another.

So it happened just as Amy had suggested. Somehow she managed to stay awake for what seemed like hours, and finally she pulled on five strings to awaken the five other girls. Ever so softly they crept up the stairs, which seemed to creak more than ever. But they made it up to the attic without being caught.

And what do you suppose they should see there? Miss Kay and all the teachers staring out the window at the comet! Amy and her friends got to watch the comet for a minute too, before anyone fully realized that there were actually six girls up here, come out of bed and up to the attic.

The teachers expressed shock and amazement, but all Miss Kay would say was, "We shall deal with this in the morning." All six girls scurried back to bed, and some of them shed a few tears of fright over what might happen in the morning to young girls who had so willfully and obviously disobeyed.

Amy didn't sleep at all. She was terribly afraid of being expelled—and then what a shame and reproach she would bring on her parents! No matter what happened, she didn't want to humiliate them.

Of course none of the mistresses doubted that Amy was the ringleader, even though several of the other girls offered to share the blame. But although Amy was punished, she was not expelled, and all the teachers and even Miss Kay forgave her.

It was at Marlborough House that Amy reached the turning point of her life. A visiting preacher, Mr. Edwin Arrowsmith, spoke to the group of girls, and his words touched Amy's heart in a way that no speaking or singing had touched it before.

She had realized for years that the Lord loved her, and she had truly thought that she had loved Him. But now, through Mr. Arrowsmith's words, she realized that this was not enough. She needed a Saviour to rescue her from death, and Jesus was that Saviour. In the few moments of quiet after the message, the Lord Jesus reached down and took another little lamb to Himself. Amy came to know Him as her own Good Shepherd.

Chapter Five
Life in Belfast

Amy had to return home from boarding school after three years because her family no longer had enough money to pay for her schooling. For that same reason, they had left Millisle and moved to Belfast, hoping that there they could find work that would pay better. Now Amy got to spend more time with her father, a godly man who made a great impression on her.

One day Mrs. Carmichael said, "Amy, dear, I do so want to get you a nice dress. Here you are already sixteen, and you don't have a single really nice dress."

"Mother, I would love to go to parties in an elegant dress. But I'm afraid that might not be wise, now that you and Father don't have much money."

"Fiddlesticks. We have enough money to buy our girl a dress. Let's at least go look in the store. I'm sure we'll see something you'll like, and I'm sure you'll look just stunning in it."

As soon as they reached the shop, the dress in the window made Amy draw in her breath. It was a beautiful, rich, royal blue. "Oh, Mother, if there were any color of dress . . ."

"Yes, yes, dear, let's try it on."

The dress fit Amy beautifully and complemented her brown eyes and hair. But still she was worried. "I just hate to think of your spending this money on me yet. Maybe in a year, when I'm seventeen, you'll have more money, and this won't be so costly for you. I can easily wait."

But in the spring of 1885, when Amy was seventeen, an unexpected tragedy hit the Carmichael home. Mr. Carmichael contracted a serious case of pneumonia. His family realized that he was extremely ill.

"Catherine," he whispered to his wife one day, "sing 'My Faith Looks Up to Thee.' "

And with a broken voice Mrs. Carmichael sang,

> My faith looks up to Thee,
> Thou Lamb of Calvary,
> Saviour divine!
> Now hear me while I pray,
> Take all my guilt away,
> O let me from this day
> Be wholly Thine!

Tears stung Amy's eyes as she listened to her mother sing and realized that her father was dying. He went to be with the Lord on April 12, a bright and beautiful Sunday morning.

Suddenly Amy was a girl no longer. Her mother needed to rely on her in many ways, and Amy became a woman.

One Sunday when Amy and her family were all walking home from church, Ernest spied an ugly old woman, clothed in rags, struggling under the burden of a heavy package. "I suppose we really ought to help her," he murmured.

"Yes, we really should," Amy answered, and she and Ernest and Alfred strode up to the woman. Ernest took the package, and Amy and Alfred each lent the woman an arm to support her. Together this way they all four continued up the street. Suddenly Amy realized that people, the other people returning from church, were looking at her, watching her act as if this ugly old woman were someone she actually knew! And here they were, helping this woman carry a package, working on the Sabbath day.

Amy's face burned with humiliation and indignation. A damp, chilly wind blew the old woman's rags against Amy's clean Sunday clothes, and she suddenly wondered why she had felt the pity to help her. She wanted to run away.

They passed one of the city fountains, and then in a flash Amy seemed to hear the words of I Corinthians 3: "Now if any man build upon this foundation gold, silver, precious stones, wood, hay, stubble; every man's work shall be made manifest: for the day shall declare it, because it shall be revealed by fire; and the fire shall try every man's work of what sort it is. . . . If any man's work shall be burned, he shall suffer loss. . . ."

Amy jumped. No, no one was around. All was the same. The same fountain, the same old woman, the same people looking with surprise at the little group. But not everything was quite the same. Now Amy's heart, rather than her face, burned with shame and humiliation. She knew that she had not done this service for the right reason. This work would not abide.

But please God, the work that she did for Him from now on would abide.

Amy so wanted to serve Jesus that she began to teach little children around Belfast whenever she could get them into groups. She started a boys' Bible study and a girls' prayer meeting. And on Sunday mornings she started a class for the girls who worked in the mill there in Belfast, girls who were so poor that they couldn't afford to wear hats to church but wore shawls instead. Just this fact alone made most respectable people not want to have anything to do with the "shawlies," but Amy Carmichael realized that they needed the Lord as much as anyone, and she ventured to train them in His Word by holding Bible studies with them. Even when Amy had to travel through parts of the city where wicked men lived, her mother knew that the Lord would protect Amy, as long as she was going about His business.

The dirty, sinful way of life that Amy saw when she visited the mill girls made her heart ache. More fervently than ever she prayed for these girls that were under her care and that thought so highly of her, praying that they might somehow, by the grace of God, grow up to be godly girls.

Still, though, Amy often felt ill at ease in her heart. In spite of her work with the shawlies, she still didn't know how she could surely live a holy life. In 1886, when she was eighteen, Amy visited some friends in Glasgow, Scotland. There she attended a series of meetings. At one of those meetings someone helped her to realize what a holy life really meant. But when

she got home, she was at first too shy to tell Mother about it.

"Amy," Mother said one day, "you're eighteen now. I would like to take you out to at least buy some material for a nice dress."

They went down to the shop once again, as they had so many months ago, and looked through the windows. One store had a bolt of beautiful blue cloth, and of course the two ladies went in there. But all of a sudden a pang shot through Amy. "Mother," she whispered urgently, "I can't do this."

"Can't? But why not, dear?"

"I can't tell you just now. But I feel that I mustn't get a party dress."

"Here we are, ladies," the red-faced, bespectacled shopman said. He was carrying several bolts of cloth, most of them varying shades of blue. "This is some of the best material I have."

"We're terribly sorry for troubling you," Mrs. Carmichael began.

"But we just realized that we cannot buy any material," Amy finished.

The shopman looked on in perplexed amazement as the two embarrassed ladies hurried out of the shop.

"Amy, tell me," asked Mother. "What is it?"

"Oh, Mother, I didn't tell you about a meeting that I went to in Glasgow. I was searching, trying so hard to figure out how to live a holy life. Even with all the work I was doing for the Lord, I still didn't feel holy. I prayed that the Lord would use one of the messages to help me. But none of the messages seemed to speak to me, somehow. But then at the end a man got up to pray, and he prayed 'O

Lord, we know that Thou art able to keep us from falling.' And in that second I understood the meaning of the holy life. It is a life in which the Lord holds me up; I don't hold myself up. And it made such a difference in my thinking that even at lunch when someone complained about the mutton chops, I thought, 'Whatever does it matter about mutton chops? The Lord is able to keep us from falling!' And ever since then, my life has seemed different. And now I just know I can't get another dress, as much as I love you and want to please you. Material things aren't as important to me as before. I feel that the Lord wants something more for me, though I don't know what it is just yet."

Chapter Six
Topsy-Turvy

Amy continued her work with the shawlies with a greater zeal than ever. The ministry grew so large, in fact, that they needed a building to meet in. Amy and all the girls prayed together for the money to buy land and build a meeting hall. When the Lord provided the money and the land at a low rental cost, they named their building The Welcome, for all who needed help, both physical and spiritual, to enter there and find hope.

Shortly after Amy's twentieth birthday, another catastrophe hit the Carmichael family. All of Mr. Carmichael's savings, which had supported his family until now, were lost. But another old friend of the family had heard of this tragic turn of events and offered Mrs. Carmichael and the girls a home and work in England.

After praying over the matter, Mrs. Carmichael decided to leave her beloved Ireland and move to England. Over the next few years, all four of Amy's brothers left for other countries to earn their living, but Amy and one sister made their plans to go with

Mrs. Carmichael to England to work for Mr. Jacob MacGill, whom they called "Uncle Jacob." Amy bade a sad farewell to her friends at The Welcome.

When she arrived in England, Uncle Jacob said, "Amy, I heard about your work with the girls back in Belfast. I would like for you to conduct a similar work with factory workers here."

Amy jumped into the work with vigor and enthusiasm. She wanted to get an apartment close to the factory so that she could have more opportunities to meet with the girls there.

Before long she found an apartment that just suited her needs. The only problem was that it was dirty and attracted rats and bugs. But Amy wasn't daunted. "I'll take care of that in no time," she said. But all her cleaning didn't make much difference; the rats and bugs kept visiting her. The whole apartment building was too filthy. Amy sighed and tried to content herself with keeping the pests away from her food.

While Amy and her mother and sister worked in Manchester, they often had time to visit a friend of the family that they had met a few years before. Mr. Robert Wilson, the founder of the Keswick Convention, had met Amy when she had attended Bible studies there when she was nineteen. He became such a great friend that they began to call him the "Dear Old Man"—the D. O. M. for short. Since Mr. Wilson's wife had died only a few years before, he was lonely and loved having visits from the Carmichael family. He grew especially fond of Amy, for she reminded him so much of his own precious daughter, who had died when she was only Amy's age.

Amy worked so hard that her health grew worse and worse. Neuralgia, a disease of the nerves, plagued her often and made her whole body ache. Sometimes, as much as she hated to stop to rest, she had to go to bed for days or even weeks at a time. After a while it became clear that she needed a rest from the hard work and needed to get away from her apartment. So the D.O.M. naturally offered her a home with his family.

Mrs. Carmichael was sad to see Amy leave Manchester, but as she knew that this move would be good for Amy and would also help the D.O.M., she consented. Amy lived with Mr. Wilson's family for three years, learning great spiritual truths from him the whole time. But those three years were not without turmoil. Mr. Wilson's sons, who were much older than Amy, thought of her as an intruder into their family. They didn't like having her around. But Mr. Wilson insisted that she remain; so she did. Amy was glad to be there, even though not everyone was glad to have her.

Amy had been with the D.O.M. two years when a burden she was carrying began to feel heavier than she could bear. For years she had felt a great desire to be a missionary in some heathen land, but because of her bad health, she had decided the Lord didn't want her to. Now she couldn't get away from it.

One day Amy got down on her knees and prayed and prayed about God's call to the mission field. "Lord, I think that You don't really want me to go," she agonized. "Here—I'll write down why." She grabbed a pen and paper. "First, my mother needs me to be near. And second, Lord, You surely want me to stay with the Dear Old Man, my second father, until he goes home to heaven. I just couldn't bear to leave him so lonely again as he was before. This is my ministry for now, isn't it?

"And maybe, Lord, by staying here when I feel the burning need to go, maybe I can be an encouragement to others, making it easier for them to go if You call.

"And finally, Lord, You know the main thought that drags on my mind. I'm not strong—my health is so unreliable. And surely You don't want a sick person on the mission field. Why, just think how much more You could do with healthy people who don't always have to be stopping and resting for weeks and months at a time the way I do. Not that I want to be this way, You know. . . . "

Amy burst into tears over the agony. Part of her seemed to say "Go"; the other part seemed to say "Stay." She didn't know what to do.

For days she dragged around listlessly. Finally she had a heart-to-heart talk with the Dear Old Man, and when she went back to her room, the Lord spoke to her as clearly as if He had used a human voice.

"Go ye."

"Truly, Lord? Is that truly what You want?" She felt about to burst into tears again.

"Go ye."

"But Lord—wait, let me look at my list again. My mother—well, my mother has already given me over to the D.O.M. She doesn't get to see me much even now. And surely my second father is wholly dedicated to the Lord. He would certainly understand. And couldn't I trust You to take care of him and relieve him of his loneliness? And the other two things—even my health, that one terrible barrier— I could trust You to take care of that, too. You are the God of miracles. Lord, I can trust You to care for all these things if I truly want Your will." She began to cry, softly this time, out of relief, as she once more heard the voice speak to her heart tenderly and reassuringly, "Go."

The next day Amy wrote a letter to her mother, telling her the story of His call, her agony, and finally her peace. Fervently she prayed that Mother would understand and be willing to surrender her to the Lord fully, to go wherever He might lead.

Amy didn't need to worry. Only a few days later a long letter arrived from her mother, reassuring her in her desire to do God's work. And the D.O.M. likewise gave his consent and did his best to help, even though he was much saddened by the thought of losing the "daughter" who had brought so much cheer into his life for two years.

Mr. Wilson's sons had a surprising reaction. After two years they had grown used to having Amy around, and now she was planning to leave. They accused her of being selfish and wanting to make their father miserable.

Other people who heard of Amy's decision shook their heads and clucked their tongues. "Are you really sure that the Lord has called you into mission work? You, with all your health problems? Maybe you're just looking for adventure. Maybe you're just being a headstrong young woman." Only a few people stood strongly behind Amy's decision to go. Was she really doing the right thing?

Chapter Seven
The Other Side of the World

It was January, 1893, and Amy had been searching a whole year for the mission field where God would have her to serve. But nothing had worked out. One door after another had been closed for her. But still she was determined.

One day Mr. Wilson said, "Amy, what about Japan? It was only four years ago that the country proclaimed freedom of religion, and I know a missionary family who went there shortly after that—"

"Mr. Wilson," Amy exclaimed, "it's so funny that you should say that! Japan is one country that I've been praying about for several days! Could you maybe write a letter to your missionary friends?"

So Mr. Wilson wrote to Rev. Barclay Buxton, asking if he might need the help that an eager young woman could provide.

"I still haven't heard from him!" Amy chafed day after day.

"Patience, child," Mr. Wilson said. "Do you think a letter from Japan can fly through the air to you?"

"But souls are dying and going to hell every day that I wait for a letter. I want to leave now! There's no time to waste."

Amy finally did decide to leave for Japan before seeing a reply from Reverend Buxton. After all these months of searching, she felt that finally she had found the place where the Lord wanted her to serve. It was arranged that she would board the ship bound for China with some other lady missionaries, wait in Shanghai for the reply from Reverend Buxton, and then sail from there to Japan.

Tearfully and painfully Amy bade farewell to her mother and the Dear Old Man on March 3 as she prepared for her six-week boat trip to Japan. For all she knew, this could be the last time she would see either one of them—she thought that she might well stay in Japan for many, many years.

"I'm willing to spend my life there." Amy managed a smile as she hugged each one. "Nothing is too precious for Jesus."

After the tears and prayers of farewell, Amy boarded the *Valetta,* the ship that would take her around Spain and through the Mediterranean Sea. This trip was pleasant enough. But about two-thirds of the way to Shanghai, the women had to change ships at Colombo, a city on the island of Ceylon, off the coast of India. She boarded the *Sutlej* to go the rest of the way to Shanghai.

All the women gingerly entered the dark little cabin where they were to live the remaining weeks of their journey.

"Bugs!" one woman cried.

"A rat!" another shrieked.

At first Amy felt just as jittery as her friends. But then she remembered the apartment where she had lived in Manchester while she worked with the factory girls. "Well, ladies," she ventured, "the Lord did tell us to give thanks in everything. I guess that includes rats and bugs."

"I feel miserable," one woman moaned. It was as if she hadn't even heard what Amy had said. "Why did I even come?"

This made Amy feel even worse than the vermin problem did. Hadn't they all come because the Lord had called them? And wasn't He the one allowing their circumstances? And wouldn't He give them grace to bear with whatever He sent their way? Amy determined not to let Satan get the better of her, even when she had to check her sheets for rat droppings every night before she went to bed.

Amy's determination paid off in spiritual benefits. She didn't know it, but the captain of the ship was watching her, knowing of the desolation of her surroundings. Day after day he saw Amy continue in her determination to give thanks and to hope in the Lord. As a result, before the ship reached Shanghai, the captain came to know the Lord as his Saviour. "My heart just sings every time I think of him," Amy wrote to her mother.

In Shanghai, to her relief, Amy found a letter from the Buxtons waiting for her, gladly inviting her to come and help them with their work.

She said good-bye to her companions and sailed across the Sea of Japan. Although she had dreamed of seeing the famous Mount Fuji looming purple and misty in the distance as she neared the coast, a storm raged around the ship as it pulled into its harbor at Shimonoseki, and she could hardly see a thing.

The Buxtons' letter had said that a missionary would be at the dock to meet her, but the only people this poor, wet Irish girl saw were slender little Japanese men, women, and children, bustling about in strange, flowing garments. They smiled at her in a friendly way, their slanted eyes seeming to make their round faces look even merrier. Short legs took short, lively steps to hurry their business along to get them out of the storm as soon as possible.

"Can someone help me?" Amy spoke loudly in English—the only language she knew. But the Japanese people, as friendly and polite as they seemed to be, could speak to her only in their own odd-sounding tongue. "Well, I'm getting wet out here. Is there at least some place I could go where I could keep dry?" She tried to gesture to indicate her meaning. Finally someone led her to a small, dark room, where she sat to wait. But instead of being filled with discouragement, Amy suddenly burst out laughing, thinking how silly she must have looked to the Japanese people and how foolish the whole situation was. Valiantly she kept trying to explain her problem to the friendly, quizzical Japanese for a whole hour. But all to no avail.

Amy felt at the point of tears. "Lord," she whispered, "the situation was funny at first. But I'm getting awfully tired now. Please send some help."

Only moments later she saw a blessedly familiar sight: Western clothing. It was an American! A wonderful, English-speaking American. He quickly sized up the situation and led Amy back outside, where the storm had let up.

"There's the great Mount Fuji!" He gestured grandly into the distance.

"It's beautiful!" Amy gasped. Her spirits lifted just at the sight of the famous mountain. The grandeur and majesty really were everything she had imagined.

"And here is your way to your missionaries' house." The man pointed to a flimsy-looking vehicle with two huge wheels and a small seat. A smiling Japanese man held two long poles, as if he were going to pull the contraption through the streets.

"What in the world is that?" Amy asked in bewilderment.

"It's the Japanese answer to a hansom cab!" The man laughed. "It's called a ricksha."

"Looks more like a rickity-sha to me," Amy quipped wryly. "Am I really supposed to ride in that?"

"Certainly. All you do is tell the 'driver' where you want to go, and he'll get you there."

"Oh, my," Amy sighed. "Well, thank you very much for your help." With her baggage all finally aboard the vehicle, Amy climbed on herself, with trepidation. She gave the name, and the smiling Japanese man nodded. With a sudden burst of energy he took off, and Amy held on to her hat and prayed the whole way to the mission compound.

The Buxtons were extremely sorry for Amy's trouble at the landing dock, but they couldn't help but laugh at her comical retelling of her misadventures there. "But, you know," Mr. Buxton said thoughtfully, "when you consider that Japan has about thirty million people and only about three thousand

Westerners, then you begin to realize what a miracle it was that the Lord sent that American along just when He did."

Later Amy and Mrs. Buxton went outside where the tree branches dripped from the recent rainfall and the birds nearly burst with song.

"I just can't get over what a beautiful land this is!" Amy bubbled. "The gorgeous cherry trees in bloom and the mountains spread over the horizon. There's nothing like it in England or Ireland, surely. England is nothing but a patch of fog this time of year! And what are these amazing flowers?" She gestured to blossoms of brilliant red, violet, and pink that were spread luxuriously through the garden.

"Those are azaleas, the pride of every Japanese home," Mrs. Buxton answered. "These people are great lovers of beauty, and spring certainly shows it. You arrived at a good time," she added. "That storm that your ship drove through had lasted two weeks."

"Oh, dear! Is that common?"

"Very common this time of year, and even more so as summer approaches. In fact, in June we often will see only five or six sunny days. Monsoons soak the country clear through. *Everything* gets wet."

Amy shivered a little, thinking of the dampness in England that had always made her bones and nerves ache.

Mrs. Buxton noticed her slight movement. "Mr. Wilson wrote in his letter to us that you suffered from neuralgia. I'm afraid that the dampness in this country won't do your condition any good at all."

"I know the Lord will care for me through anything like that," Amy answered blithely. "Tell me about the people here. I know I have a lot to learn—they certainly aren't British!"

"No, far from it," Mrs. Buxton agreed with a laugh as the two women went back inside. "There are some things you'll have to get used to, such as the raw fish that they eat—"

"Raw fish!" Amy made a face.

"Yes, they consider it quite a delicacy. That's only one of the many things that are different about the Japanese people. You'll find out more about them as you work and learn. But the main thing you need to know about now is their religion. Most of the people we work with are Buddhists. They believe that the man-god they call Buddha had the secret to eternal happiness. You'll see statues of him everywhere whenever we travel. They think themselves far too 'intelligent' to believe in a Creator. They'll say, 'Who created Him?' So instead they believe in an eternal cycle of birth, death, and rebirth, called reincarnation. How *that* got started they don't say. Everything in your future life depends on how you live in this life— your good deeds against your bad ones, you know. So if a man isn't good, he may come back as— horrors!—a woman."

Amy laughed at Mrs. Buxton's funny expression. "I see they don't have too high an opinion of women here."

"No, but we manage fine anyway. They also believe—in theory, at least—that if you're really bad, in your next life you might not be a human being at all but some sort of animal."

"But where does the cycle end?"

"For most of them, the end of the cycle seems like an impossibility. Only by overcoming their selfish desires can any of them reach eternal happiness and end their cycle. Their hope for 'heaven' is based entirely on what they can do for themselves, not what any god has done for them."

"But then why do they worship the statues?" Amy wanted to know. "It seems that they would scorn *any* god."

"Well, you have to know the difference between the 'elite' Buddhist and the 'peasant' Buddhist. The well-educated group does scorn worship of idols. But they think that the masses have to have them to understand the religion. Besides," Mrs. Buxton lifted her hands in a gesture of despair, "there are so many different old religions woven into the fabric of their Buddhism that it takes years of study to figure it out. We've only just begun to understand it. Some Japanese claim to have over eight *million* different gods besides Buddha!"

"Eight million?" Amy gasped. "No wonder they're confused!"

"And they don't consider it the least bit unfaithful to worship whichever ones they choose—in addition to Buddha, that is." Mrs. Buxton shrugged her shoulders slightly. "They aren't even willing to admit that there is such a thing as sin, and yet they spend all their lives trying to conquer it."

"Oh, my," Amy sighed. "This really is a dark land. They desperately need the light of the gospel."

"And we're so glad to have you here to help us send it out, Amy." Mrs. Buxton smiled. "You're an answer to our prayer."

"But I need to get started witnessing now!" Amy declared. "There's not a moment to lose. Souls are dying and going to hell!"

Chapter Eight
The Kimono and the Fox God

Even though Amy needed to spend many hours a day in language study, the Buxtons wanted her to have opportunities to witness too. So after only a few weeks, they assigned Misaki San, a Christian Japanese girl, to interpret for Amy as she went about Japan to witness to the people there.

One day as Amy prepared to go out with Misaki San, her neuralgia seemed to be plaguing her more than ever. The day was unseasonably cold, and it seemed that every bone ached.

"It is the custom for women missionaries to wear the Japanese kimono when they go calling on the Japanese women," Misaki San said gently as they prepared to leave.

Amy sighed heavily. "But those things are so drafty, and really I'm quite chilly, Misaki San. My English clothes won't get in the way of our witnessing, now, will they?" she added with a smile.

"One cannot tell these things beforehand," Misaki San murmured.

Amy felt especially conscious of the staring eyes this time as she and Misaki San walked through the streets of the city. The people still had not gotten used to seeing this English lady in her strange clothes.

The old, sick woman that they went to see seemed interested in the new message she heard, with Amy speaking and Misaki San translating. But as it turned out, just as Amy was ready to say, "Will you repent and put your trust in the Lord Jesus," the old woman caught sight of Amy's fur gloves. She reached out a wrinkled hand to touch them. "What are these?" she asked, intrigued. She forgot about the message of the gospel that she had come so close to receiving.

Misaki San did not look at Amy, whose face burned as she tried to draw the woman's attention back to Jesus. On the way home, Amy felt hot tears of remorse and humility streaming down her face. "Never, never, Lord willing," she told her faithful interpreter, "will I risk so much for so little." When she arrived back at the house, she took off her English dress and gloves and put on the Japanese kimono, determined to do her best from then on not to distract people's eyes from the Lord.

Amy spent more months working and witnessing. But one day she had an opportunity to help in a way that comes rarely in the life of the average missionary. She and Misaki San heard of a man in a certain village who was in a desperate condition.

"He goes wild and throws himself around," the villagers explained. "He tries to kill people with his bare hands. The spirit of the fox is living in him."

Misaki San explained to Amy that the fox god was one of the main gods that the Japanese people worshiped. If anyone angered him, they believed, he worked his revenge powerfully and terribly.

"It is a demon," Amy answered with certainty. "But our Lord Jesus is stronger than any demon. Misaki San and I will go there."

Amy and Misaki San prayed fervently, claiming the promise "in My name they will cast out devils." Then they ventured to the house of the afflicted man.

The religious leaders of the village had tried every prayer and incantation they knew. But still the "fox spirit" controlled the man. So now they had resorted to the last thing they could think of to do: they had tied his arms and legs down to wooden boards and had set glowing coals on different parts of his body. These glowing coals, they hoped, would drive out the spirit.

Amy was appalled when she entered the tiny room and saw the man stretched out, dazed from the pain. She tried to hide her feelings, though, as she spoke to his weeping wife. "We know that everything the men of the village have done has not cast out this demon," she said. "But the power of our Lord Jesus can cast it out."

As soon as he heard the name of the Lord, the possessed man jumped up out of his daze, snarling and yelling. If he hadn't been tied to the wooden boards, he would have attacked Amy and Misaki San right there. As the men around him tried to control him, the two missionaries almost ran as they left the room. The man's wife followed, waiting to hear their explanation for her husband's sudden rage.

Amy felt almost helpless. Why had this happened? Wasn't the Lord Jesus more powerful than demons?

Of course He was. No matter what the man's reaction had been at first, she knew that Jesus still had the power to make him well again. Suddenly she felt as if the Spirit of God were speaking to her. She boldly said to the woman, "Our Lord Jesus will still cast out the spirit. We will go and pray until He has. Tell us when it happens." Then the two women quietly went on their way back to the mission compound.

Not even an hour had passed before a messenger came to tell the women that the man was well. The demon was gone, and he was sleeping. "Misaki San," Amy whispered, "nothing is too hard for our Lord!"

The next day the man asked to see the two missionaries. He lay in bed, recovering from his burns, clothed and looking like a proper man. "Tell me," he said quietly, "tell me how you sent the fox spirit away."

Amy hastened to make one thing clear. "Sir, we did not cast out the spirit. The Lord Jesus did it. He is the greatest and most powerful God."

"Greater and more powerful than Buddha?" the man murmured. "Yes, He must be, for with all their many prayers to Buddha, the men of this village only made the fox inside me laugh with scorn. Tell me more about this God Jesus."

So Amy and Misaki San talked to him for hours that day and many days after, telling him the stories of how Jesus had come to earth, how He had died for the sins of mankind, and how He lives again, victorious forever and supremely powerful. The man, snatched from the grip of Buddhism, came to know Jesus as his own Saviour from sin.

Chapter Nine
"Just Four Souls, Lord"

Little did Amy know how short her stay in Japan would be. But the Lord used her mightily in the few months that she worked with the Buxtons. An experience that Amy had in another village, called Hirose, gives a good example of her boldness in believing the Lord's promises.

The Buddhists of Japan were a hard people to win. If a missionary saw only five souls come to know the true God in one year, he wasn't discouraged. Amy knew this. But she believed in praying first to know the will of God and then praying that His will would be done, confident of the answer she would receive.

As she and Misaki San prepared to visit the Buddhist village of Hirose, where there were only a few Christians, Amy desperately desired to know what she could ask of God, to pray for His will in the visit. Finally she felt led to trust the Lord to bring one soul to Himself on this visit.

A young girl weaving silk stopped long enough to listen intently as the two missionaries told her the story of Jesus. She came to know Him then.

In the cold Japanese winter, Amy's neuralgia hit her hard. Much to her chagrin, she had to stay in bed for a month after that first visit to Hirose.

When Amy was well enough to go out again, she prayed once more. This time she felt led to ask for two souls. Again the Lord answered her prayer—the young silk weaver brought one person to hear who accepted the Lord. The other was an old woman. Amy and Misaki San left all three of these new Christians in the hands of one of the few godly people in that village who could help them to grow. Two weeks later the two women prepared to go back again.

"Misaki San," Amy began.

"Yes, Miss Carmichael?"

"I cannot help but feel that the Lord would give us four souls this time."

"Four souls? That is far more than most people see won at one time. Are you sure?"

"I feel very sure. I have prayed and prayed about it."

"We must tell the others, then, so that they will be behind us in prayer for this matter. If you are sure."

"I am sure."

Much prayer followed the two women as they left this time. Four souls in a Buddhist village would be a true miracle.

Through the freezing snow Amy and Misaki San rode in their ricksha, the wheels careening at every turn because the "driver" hurried as fast as he could in the cold. The bitter winds seemed to bite through every layer of Amy's thick clothing. The pain in her nerves grew stronger. She hugged her weary limbs.

"Why *can't* he hurry a little faster?" she chafed. "We have to get there! We mustn't waste any time!"

When they finally arrived in Hirose, Amy and Misaki San visited house after house, but not one person seemed interested this time. Amy hadn't felt this discouraged in many days.

"Ha ha!" a voice seemed to shout in her ear. "No souls for you in Hirose this time! How foolish of you to think that the Lord would actually give you four. You'd have been better off if you'd never mentioned it to anyone!"

"Misaki San," Amy said suddenly.

"Yes, Miss Carmichael?"

"I can't help but be afraid that . . . that maybe I misunderstood the Lord's will about four souls. Maybe I was foolish and presumptuous. I can be that way sometimes, you know." She looked down in discouragement.

"Miss Carmichael, did you truly want the Lord's will?"

"Yes, oh yes, more than anything. No matter what it was."

"Then He will not lead you astray. The four souls are here somewhere. Let us wait and see who will come to the meeting tonight."

Amy nodded without answering. She didn't expect many people at the meeting.

Indeed, not many came. Those who did come seemed distracted and uninterested. The same presence that had whispered in Amy's ear to discourage her seemed to be working extra hard here to draw the attention of the listeners in all different directions.

Amy was almost in tears, beginning to abandon all hope, wanting to rush out and lose herself in the snow.

But suddenly she sensed a difference in the spirit of the meeting. The mocking presence seemed to have left; a new divine presence seemed to have taken its place.

"I want to believe." It was the voice of one of the women who had seemed the most distracted earlier in the evening. Amy and Misaki San carefully explained to the woman about the one who had died for her sins, and she took the Lord Jesus as her Saviour. Shortly after, the woman's son came in, and he too was saved.

The Lord brought no more sheep into the fold at that meeting, but Amy and Misaki San rejoiced anyway. Amy's spirit felt renewed, knowing that she really hadn't misread the Lord's will and that indeed the other two souls were in Hirose somewhere—to be brought to the Lord before the women left the next day.

"Look, Misaki San—don't some Christians live in that house? Let's stop in and tell them the good news."

As the two missionaries related the story to their Japanese brothers and sisters, one of them said, "There is another who would like to hear of Jesus. Could you perhaps speak with her at your honorable convenience?" And so another sister was brought into the family of God.

"One more soul, and we will have our four!" Amy exclaimed.

The Lord brought the fourth in the unexpected return of one man's wife from another village the next day. She had wanted to be a "Jesus-person" for some time and was ready to listen with eagerness as the two women explained salvation to her. Then back to Matsuye they journeyed, praising the Lord.

"Misaki San," Amy said suddenly, "I just thought of something."

"Yes, Miss Carmichael?"

"Why, it's December 16! It's my birthday! I've never gotten a sweeter birthday present than the four that the Lord gave us this visit!"

*　　　*　　　*

Again Amy had to rest. A month and a half went by before the women planned to venture out to Hirose again. It was the end of January.

"Misaki San."

"Yes, Miss Carmichael?"

"I know you won't scoff at this—but for two weeks now the Lord has been impressing me that we should pray for eight souls in Hirose this time."

"*Eight* souls, Miss Carmichael?"

"Yes, I know it sounds foolish, but I have been struggling with it for two weeks, and the more I struggle, the more convinced I am that it is truth."

"Then let us tell the other missionaries."

The reaction from the others wasn't good. A missionary looked at her seriously. "One soul, Amy—that was good to pray for. Two souls—that was even better. Four souls, I'll admit, we were skeptical about, but the Lord provided them. But *eight* souls? No, no. That is not faith; it's presumption. How terrible it would be to claim something as God's will and then find that thing not provided! If you just pray for a blessing, you won't be disappointed. Let's just pray for a blessing."

Amy felt miserable. "Please believe me. When I was praying for only four souls, I felt fear and trembling about it. I wouldn't ever pray for eight souls in my own strength. But don't you see—the Lord has wrestled with me about this! I *have* to pray for eight souls!"

One older Christian interrupted what the younger ones were about to say. "The Lord is with her," he said simply. "The Lord speaks to her. Let us believe and pray." He opened his Bible and read Jeremiah 32:27. "Is anything too hard for the Lord?" he asked. Then he prayed. Around the room the others prayed too. Finally they all agreed that Amy and Misaki San should leave for Hirose while the Christians in Matsuye prayed along with them for eight souls.

Once again the Lord provided. One by one, He brought eight precious new sheep out of sin and into His fold.

"Misaki San," Amy said, "my faith has been tested. His faithfulness has been proven. Praise His name!"

Chapter Ten
India at Last

Amy's neuralgia finally put her to bed for a long time. In the spring of that year, 1894, she was so sick that the doctor advised her to leave Japan. "The climate here isn't good for you," he decided. Many friends from back home wrote letters trying to persuade Amy to return to England, but since she had been in Japan only a little over a year, the stubborn Irish woman felt reluctant to leave the mission field so soon.

The doctor advised Amy to go to China for a while to recover, which she did, fully expecting to return to Japan in only a few weeks. But the Lord led in a different direction. She spent several months ministering on the island of Ceylon near India, all the while struggling with the advice from friends all around her who kept saying, "You need to go back to England for the sake of your health." But it wasn't until she got a message that the D.O.M. had suffered a stroke that she finally did return to his home.

While Amy was in England spending time with her slowly recovering D.O.M., she received a letter from a friend. This woman, who had heard of Amy's physical troubles in Japan, worked in South India. "The climate here is just delightful," she wrote. "I'm sure that it would even be good for you, dear Amy. And since India is under British control, there are many English missionaries and other things that will remind you of home. Please consider coming to Bangalore, even for just a short time. I'm sure you could have a tremendous ministry here."

"Amy," Mother said one night when she was visiting with her daughter, "this sounds as if it may be where the Lord wants you."

"No, I don't think so, Mother," Amy answered a little stubbornly. "It sounds far too easy to me."

The D.O.M. raised himself up from the bed. "Don't be foolish, child," he said. "The climate is such that you wouldn't have to go to bed with a raging fever every other week. That means that you could spend more time among the people winning them to the Lord. Does that mean that the Lord doesn't want you there?"

Amy looked chagrined at her hasty words. "Of course, I hadn't prayed over the matter at all when I answered you," she apologized. "Maybe the Lord really does want me there."

As it turned out, no doctor would approve Amy for return to Japan anyway. So after much prayer, she decided to request from the mission board that she be allowed to go to Bangalore, South India, instead. Unrolling a blue banner that showed on it the words that had become her motto—"Nothing too precious for Jesus"—she spoke before a group of them. They gave their approval that night.

Amy was able to celebrate the D.O.M.'s seventieth birthday with him, but it was the last birthday of his that she would ever see. On October 11, 1895, she bade farewell to her family and to the Dear Old Man and set sail for a country that she had never seen. Little did she know it then, but she was to spend the rest of her life there—over fifty-five years.

Amy arrived in Bangalore about a month after she had left England. She had a raging fever. Dengue, or bone-break fever as it is called, usually also causes depression, and Amy was no exception. For days she sat or lay in her room at the mission compound. Even when she was feeling fairly well physically, she felt terribly depressed.

One afternoon Amy lay gazing at the calendar. It was December 16, her twenty-eighth birthday, but of course no one at the mission compound knew that. The other missionaries were kind, but none of them, at least not so far, had become a personal friend to Amy as Misaki San had been. "I don't know anyone here," she sighed to herself. "I'm just a burden to them. I'm sure they wish I would go back to England. Or maybe die." She rubbed her forehead. "Lord," she sobbed, "this is so different from two years ago. Do You remember that, Lord? My birthday two years ago—that was the day in Hirose when You gave me four souls. What a happy birthday that was. But this one is just miserable, Father. Do You really want me here at all?"

It seemed then that even the Lord wouldn't answer her. Amy sighed loudly and gazed out the window. The land was hot, dry, and dusty. Amy sighed again as she thought what Japan would be like at this time of year—the lovely white snow falling and crystallizing the trees, the great Mount Fuji standing guard on the horizon. Somehow she forgot how that same winter weather had made her nerves ache so. Here, where the thermometer never fell below sixty-five degrees, her birthday seemed a stranger to her.

Still, the land of India had a certain kind of exotic charm. It was different from Japan, of course, but was still lovely in its own way. Although she couldn't see any mountains on the horizon as she had in Japan, she knew from map studies that the mountains were out there somewhere. Stories of thieves that liked to hide in those hills and waylay travelers had made her spine tingle. But she had also heard that those same hills were the ideal place for weary missionaries to cool off in the summer months when the heat became unbearable.

What she did see on the horizon was an endless row of mango and tamarind trees, half hiding the hutlike houses of the city. And closer to her window ran a well-traveled road. This was what held her attention. Not the road itself, really—it was as colorless as the rest of the land—but the people traveling on it. As Amy gazed, she saw snatches of scarlet, pink, purple, gold, and pristine white flash by her. Maybe it was because their land had so little color, but the people of India valued color in all their clothing and all over their houses, in their shops and in their temples.

"Well, we'll see. If the Lord will just help me to get over my depression, I'll trust Him to show me whether or not He really does want me in India at all."

Amy did finally recover from the illness as well as the depression that the illness caused. Soon she was back to her old self. Even though she had to spend almost all of her time studying the complicated Tamil language, she still managed to have some time for fun. And when she had her fun, she tried not to let the stiffness of some of the missionaries discourage her. In fact, when she got a pony, she decided to race with a carriage—a carriage that belonged to the representative of the Queen of England!

"You say you are twenty-eight years old, do you?" sniffed a missionary woman. "You act like a child, racing that pony through the streets."

"But I didn't mean to do anything wrong," Amy hurried to explain. "It's just that after getting over that dreadful fever and being cooped up in my room for so long, it feels so lovely to be able to—"

"It's utterly childish, that's what it is." The woman ignored everything Amy had said. "If you want to know how to behave like a true lady, I could give you lessons in that!"

Amy's Irish temper flared up in a moment. She wanted to burst out, "You stuffy old woman! You probably never had a day of fun in your life! If being a 'true lady' means being like you, I hope I never become one!" But the words never left her mouth. A voice spoke to her heart, so clearly that it was as if someone were standing by her side, but she knew that the voice came from inside her heart. "See in this a chance to die," it said.

Amy struggled for a moment more with the pride inside her that longed to leap out. Finally she said meekly, "Yes, ma'am. I'm sorry."

"See to it that you don't let it happen again, young lady. Racing with the Queen's ambassador like that could be a bad testimony."

Amy bit her lip and excused herself to her room, where she burst into tears. Finally she controlled herself and whispered, "Yes, she's right. I don't know enough about India to know but that racing with the Queen's ambassador just might be a bad testimony." Then she giggled. "But it *was* a lot of fun!"

Amy struggled to be the kind of young missionary that would be acceptable to her elders at Bangalore. But she felt discouraged at not getting to know more about the people she was supposed to be here to minister to. There were so many British missionaries here that she didn't feel as needed as she had in Japan. The older ones did the missionary work. She just had to study her Tamil grammar.

One night as the missionary ladies were all sitting around sedately sewing, one of them casually asked, "Does anyone here know of any Indian Christians that will work without getting paid?"

The room was silent for a moment as Amy waited expectantly for an answer. Finally one said, "I must confess that I can't think of one."

"Well, you know what they say," another woman said with a chuckle.

The others laughed and fell silent. They all must have known what it was that they say. Amy, though, was burning with curiosity.

"No, I don't," she said.

"Don't what, child?"

"I don't know what they say. What is it?"

"Oh, it's an old Indian saying. 'Say *money,* and a corpse will open its mouth.' " The speaker made such a funny expression when she spoke that everyone laughed again.

"I know that that's true of most of the Indian people. The street sellers always hold their palms up for you to put money in them. But surely that isn't true of *Christian* Indians?" Amy protested.

"Oh, but it is. And unfortunately there doesn't seem to be any way to change it. Not that we mind paying them, you know. It's just that so many of them want more than we can afford to give. It seems that they'd rather not work at all than work for less than they think they deserve." The woman sighed.

"It's funny," one woman put in. "An Indian who wants to achieve holiness can have the determination to sit with his palms clenched until his fingernails grow out the back of his hands. But the average Indian won't do a thing unless he knows he'll be paid handsomely for it."

As the women began to talk of other things, Amy said no more. But she did a lot of thinking. Could it be that the reason the Indian Christians weren't more spiritually minded was that the missionaries weren't praying for them as they should have been? Since she was one of the youngest members of the group, Amy felt out of place asking such a question out loud, but she asked it in her heart again and again that night. "Please, Lord," she prayed, "when You give me Indians to work with me, let them not put anything before You."

Chapter Eleven
Tinnevelly District

One day a special missionary speaker, Mr. Thomas Walker, was scheduled to speak in a place where Amy was visiting. Even though Amy wasn't feeling well, she was determined to go hear him speak. "I've heard so much about him," she explained to herself. "And if he doesn't turn out to be any good, well, I have my Tamil grammar book here to study."

But Mr. Walker, the well-known missionary from the district of India called Tinnevelly, held Amy's interest for the entire evening. Afterwards she spoke to him about some of her problems with the Tamil grammar.

"Mr. Walker," she began, "I really think that I could learn this language much more easily if I went to live with the Indian people in a mud hut, don't you? I mean, just studying it from a book and listening to other foreigners speak it doesn't seem like the quickest or best way to learn. And souls are dying and going to hell every minute. There's really no time to waste."

Mr. Walker studied Amy's pale cheeks for a moment before answering. "I think," he began slowly, "that living in a mud hut would be a foolish thing for a girl like you—your frail health wouldn't stand it."

"Well, who does he think he is," Amy's thoughts burned within her, "to talk about my health in such a way? What can he possibly know about it?" She decided then and there that she didn't like this man at all.

"I do have an idea, though," the missionary continued as Amy only half-listened. "Bangalore is full of English-speaking people, as you have implied. If you were to come work in Tinnevelly, you would have more contact with the native Indians, and I could teach you the Tamil language."

"Thank you for the invitation," Amy answered, hoping to sound polite. She mulled over the idea, finally deciding that although she didn't like Mr. Walker, she thought his wife was quite charming, and she found that she too suffered from health problems and could perhaps be an encouragement to Amy. Besides, it probably would be a good idea to learn Tamil from one so knowledgeable.

Amy prayed about the matter and, in December of 1896, one year after she had arrived, she got permission to go with Mr. and Mrs. Walker to Palamcottah, the area of Tinnevelly where they lived and worked. This was where almost all of the Christian work in Tinnevelly was done. Amy lived there with them for several months, doing some work but mostly struggling with her Indian grammar. As her teacher, Mr. Walker, helped her, she began to see that she had misjudged him earlier. He became like an older brother to her.

"Mr. Walker," Amy said one day, "something about our mission work in India bothers me, and I've prayed about it, and I really feel that the Lord wants me to do something about it." She hesitated.

"Yes, young lady, what is it?"

"When I was in Japan, I found that the ministry was greatly hindered by my wearing English clothes instead of a kimono. And here in India I feel the same way—I should be dressing like a native woman, wearing a sari, so that the people I speak to won't be as suspicious of me. But no missionary here does that. What do you think?"

"I think it is a matter to pray over, but it sounds as if you have spoken a bit of wisdom here."

As it turned out, Mr. and Mrs. Walker were two of the few missionaries who stood behind Amy in her decision to dress like a native woman. But even in the midst of the controversy, Amy felt sure she was doing the right thing. She remembered the fur gloves in Japan and the lesson she had learned through them.

One day Amy returned from one of her brief witnessing forays, laughing in embarrassment. "I must need to get back to my grammar books," she said to her teacher. "Somehow I think I never learned the Tamil word for *home*. I was trying to describe our heavenly home to a woman, and I couldn't say it!"

"And with good reason," Mr. Walker replied. "There is no word in the Tamil for *home*. The closest you can come is *house*."

"But why is that? How do they describe their . . . well, their homes!"

"They don't have homes. A home, in the English meaning of the word, is a place where love is. Love in a Hindu household is the exception rather than the rule. The house to these people is just a place to stay; the family is often considered nothing more than a necessary evil. So you must make do without that wonderful word. But Amy," he continued, "Mrs. Walker and I have made a decision. You know that we've been somewhat discontent here in Palamcottah because so much missionary work is going on here already. We've decided to move to Pannaivilai, where fewer natives have heard the gospel. We would like you to go with us and work with us there, if you are willing."

It was a matter for prayer once again. Amy requested permission of the missionaries back in Bangalore, and they consented.

In Pannaivilai, as it turned out, Amy was able to start a mission work similar to The Welcome. She began a Bible study with some converts who were already there. And as she worked with them, others joined the group too.

The most faithful of her Indian workers, Ponnammal, came to be Amy's close friend and worked with her for many years. She helped Amy lead and teach the women's Bible-study group. From this group, the Women's Band was formed to work full-time to take the gospel to their people. The Band became known as the "Starry Cluster" to the other Indians. In the cooler months, these women traveled around the district together, teaching women and children about the Lord.

But one problem here in India was similar to a common problem back in England. Sometimes people would claim to be saved but would show no fruit. They would continue with many of their Hindu customs. Amy prayed fervently that the women in her Band would show fruit as true believers.

Her prayer was answered when one day all the women in the Starry Cluster trooped into her room one by one. "Please take our pay," Ponnammal said. "We want to give it to the Lord's work." As Amy looked up in disbelief, Ponnammal continued. "We see the need to tell about Jesus to the people in so many villages—the people that still think that their good works will let them live again and again—but we see that there is not enough money. So we have decided that we want to work for the Lord without receiving pay. We will be glad to work for whatever He decides to give."

Amy remembered the missionaries in Bangalore talking about the Indian Christians that they knew— "Say *money* and a corpse will open its mouth." And now here was a group of women who didn't let money stand in the way of their service for their King.

Some time later members of the Starry Cluster made another unexpected decision. It had to do with the jewels that they all wore.

No Indian woman would dare be seen without huge clusters of pearls around her ears and a disc of real gold hanging from the lobes, or a sparkling gem in her nose and several gold necklaces, bracelets, and rings, inset with more sparkling jewels. All this, even if the woman didn't have food to eat. It was unthinkable to even consider selling her jewels for bread. Unthinkable! Any Indian woman knew that everyone would scorn her and deride her if she wore no jewels. Her jewels were her dowry, the indicators of her husband's wealth. To the Indian it was far better to leave your children and grandchildren deeply in debt than to die without jewels.

Amy knew that the jewels these women wore were worth a great amount of money that could be used for the Lord's work, but she didn't want to bring up the matter herself. She prayed and waited for the Lord to speak to them.

It all began when one woman's husband suggested that she give up her jewels for her new life. Give up her jewels? Did she dare face that kind of scoffing? She did it, but grudgingly.

Then Ponnammal thought more and more about the matter and decided that it was the right thing for her to do too, because of all her Saviour had done for her. She was willing to face the scorn that the Hindus would undoubtedly heap upon her head. One by one, other members of the Band realized that their jewels were a source of vanity for them. If they got rid of them, they could concentrate on their service for the Lord even more.

Amy could hardly believe her eyes when several members of her band presented their jewels to her, asking her to sell them and use the money for the Lord's work. "But what will your people say?" she asked, taken aback.

"It does not matter what our people will say," Ponnammal answered. "What matters is that this is what our Lord has told us to do."

The others agreed. One said, "If I had loved my Saviour more, I would have loved my jewels less."

No one would have been surprised if the Hindus had been upset at the sacrifice the Starry Cluster had made. But no one was prepared for the storm of protest that they did receive—not from the Hindus, but from the other Indian Christians! "Scandalous!" they charged. "An outrage! To think that they would give up their dowry and go about with absolutely no jewels!"

But the Hindus were impressed with the devotion of these Christian women. "A religion for which they would give up their jewels," they concluded, "must be a true religion indeed."

Another advantage came of giving up the jewels, an advantage that not even Amy had anticipated. Now the women could travel together at night because thieves knew that the members of the Starry Cluster had no jewels that could be stolen! They were able to spend more time than ever in spreading the good news of their Saviour, Jesus Christ.

Chapter Twelve
A Way of Life

The bandy that Amy and Ponnammal had to ride to get anywhere in India reminded Amy a little of the rickshas she had used in Japan. The bandy had four wheels instead of two, and a pair of oxen pulled it instead of a man, but the ride was just as bumpy and jolting—and not much faster.

"Everybody, come and see!" The two women saw a little Indian girl run around from hut to hut in the small Hindu village. "It is truly an appalling spectacle! It is a great white man!"

Amy looked around for a moment before realizing that the "great white man" the girl referred to was Amy herself.

"She is not a man—she has on a sari! Only women wear that."

"He is too a man. See, he has on a man's turban. And besides, have you ever seen a white *woman?*"

Amy almost burst out laughing at this conversation. How she wished she didn't have to wear that silly turban, but she would faint in the heat otherwise.

"You really are a woman! A white woman wearing a turban! What an appalling spectacle!"

Amy whispered to Ponnammal, "Did you know that in England they think that women missionaries over here are looked upon as divine goddesses? Just wait till I tell them that I was referred to as an 'appalling spectacle'!"

Some mothers shooed their children inside at the sight of the missionary women. "Come!" one mother cried at a curious boy. "Do you not know that they get a hundred rupees for getting one of us to follow their way? Come!"

"Where do they ever get such notions?" Amy mused in bewilderment as she climbed down from the bandy. She looked all around at the little village they had come to. Apparently it was quite religious. Several stone shrines dotted the landscape around the huts, each shrine surrounded by dozens of idols.

Amy was relieved when a kind woman invited them into her hut out of the heat. There the "great white man" removed her turban to prove once and for all that she was really a woman.

As her eyes grew accustomed to the darkness, Amy saw several women sitting around on mats, some old, some young, some working at weaving, some just sitting and chewing on something. Most of them had slickly oiled hair parted in the middle and pulled back in a knot at the nape of the neck, as was the custom of Indian women. They all wore saris as Amy did, draped over one shoulder and pulled around the waist.

A cow was settled down in the back of the hut, lazily swatting flies with its tail.

"Won't you have some betel?" an Indian woman urged.

Amy looked at the big leaf with nut and lime rolled up in it. She watched the other women take big bites, chew for a while, and then spit it out. They seemed to be enjoying themselves immensely.

Hesitantly she took a leaf. Then she said, "Thank you so much, but it is not my country's custom to eat betel." And she returned it.

The women seemed satisfied. After chewing for a few moments longer, they began to ply her and Ponnammal with questions. "Why don't you wear jewels? Where is your family? Why have you left them all to come here?"

That was Amy's opportunity. "We have come here to tell the good news of the great God who became man," she explained with animation. "He came to earth to take the penalty for our sins." For several minutes she continued to explain, while Ponnammal occasionally helped her with the difficult language.

But the more Amy talked, the more discouraged she became. For the women simply stared at her. "Lord, speak to them," she prayed urgently. But all the women just continued to munch on their betel leaves and stare.

Finally one woman said, "Our husbands decide our religion for us." And that seemed to be that.

Amy and Ponnammal left. One old woman followed them out of the hut. "It is a nice religion you have," she remarked. "But it is mistaken. What religion could be right that would make us break our caste? I could never leave the caste into which I was born."

The woman turned and trudged back into the darkness of the hut.

When they were out of sight, Amy turned to Ponnammal. "Caste, caste, that's all they live for!" she cried in frustration.

"Indeed you are right," Ponnammal agreed. "All their lives revolve around caste. Many of them would rather die than break it. They must find, as I did, that Jesus is worth far more than caste."

Amy's mind went back to the time when Mr. Walker was first explaining to her about caste. "It is probably our biggest hindrance to spreading the gospel here in India," he'd said.

"But where in the world did such an idea come from?" Amy demanded.

Mr. Walker explained in his patient way. "You have to understand the history of Hinduism to understand caste. And even then," he added thoughtfully, "even then we Europeans can never fully understand it. "You know that Hinduism teaches reincarnation, just as Buddhism does."

"Yes, I remember that," Amy said. "That's what makes them think that all life is equally valuable— that it's just as wrong to kill a fly as it is to kill a person. Because that fly might be some dead relation."

"Right. But that is only in theory, of course. In practice they kill, sometimes with no thought or compunction. And you know that the other side of the coin is that if a person suffers great hardship here on earth, they believe that it is simply his fate, that he is suffering for the sins that he committed in some past life."

"Yes."

"Well, all these heathen beliefs led to the development of the caste system. Hindus decided that some people must be better than others, with the priests, or Brahmins at the top, on down through the warriors, the farmers, the merchants, and so on. Down to the outcastes, who aren't even considered to be in a caste at all. If a man is born a Brahmin, then they believe he must have lived a worthy life the last time around. And if someone is born an outcaste, then no one needs to feel sorry for him, because it's his own fault. He was wicked in his last life. The caste system is further complicated by the fact that these groups have been divided into hundreds and hundreds of subgroups, and most castes are never permitted to mix with any other in any way, not eating, not touching, and certainly not marrying."

"Well, I would think that anyone in any of the lower castes would be happy to abolish the caste system. They aren't allowed to do anything with their lives—to make anything of themselves."

"Well," Mr. Walker conceded, "have you noticed that almost all of our converts are of the lower castes? That is no coincidence. But still, sister Amy, you don't see that caste is more than just a social division. It's a way of life. Even for a low-caste pot-maker—if he were to be saved—it is most likely that everyone in his caste would turn on him. He would be scorned forever, and no Hindu would ever buy his pots. And pottery is all he has known his entire life! His father was a potter; his grandfather was a potter. It's unthinkable for him to try to do anything else. So when he turns his back on his caste, he turns his back on everything he has ever known in this life and faces a world full of unknowns."

Amy shook her head as she thought of those words Mr. Walker had spoken some months before. She brought her mind back to the present to hear Ponnammal saying, "Shall we go in here?"

"I suppose we should. You know, Ponnammal, sometimes I wonder why women don't jump at the chance to shed their chains of inferiority and slavery in Hinduism and obtain equality in Christianity. But then . . . other times I can see it. They'd have to give up everything."

"Yes," Ponnammal answered with the knowing look of one who had experienced it. "Everything."

Chapter Thirteen
From House to House

Amy and Ponnammal stood outside the next hut and clapped as Indians do to announce their presence. "Come in, come in!" they heard. Here they found two young women and one old one who were genuinely interested in hearing the good news of salvation. After listening in rapt attention for a whole hour, one of the young women said, "Please, come back every day and tell us more."

"Oh, how I wish we could!" Amy answered. "We can come back again, but we cannot come every day."

"But why not?"

"There are hundreds of villages, and thousands of women, and they all need to hear about Jesus, and there are so few of us to tell. . . ." Amy felt suddenly filled with frustration. Why were there so few of them among so many?

The old woman shook her head. "I believe what you tell us," she said slowly. "And maybe these young ones can follow. But for me it is too late. I cannot break my caste now. Where would I go? What would

I do? You came too late for me. Why didn't you come sooner?"

Amy struggled for a reply. But even as she spoke, she felt that her answer wasn't good enough. Why *hadn't* someone come sooner to tell? When the little children entered and demanded attention, Amy and Ponnammal left with regret.

As they approached the next house, Ponnammal said, "The Lord sent us those women for encouragement."

"Yes," Amy answered slowly. "And rebuke."

One young woman was sitting in front of the house they approached. She eyed them carefully. "I have seen you walking from house to house," she said. "You are here to tell us about the next life."

Amy hesitated as the three of them entered the darkened interior. How she defined the next life and how this woman defined it would be two different things.

But the woman didn't wait for an answer. "I plan to make a pilgrimage to the sacred Ganges River someday," she boasted. "Then in the next life I will come back as a man!"

She burst out laughing, and other laughter accompanied hers. Amy's eyes adjusted to the darkness to see several women, all adorned, as was customary for Indian women, with hundreds of rupees' worth of jewels—bracelets, armbands, necklaces, earrings, and nose-rings. Their laughter indicated that they must not have a very high regard for the men in their lives.

Another woman spoke as she pounded out a huge slab of cow dung that she planned to dry later for fuel. "Are you married or widowed?"

"I am a widow," said Ponnammal.

"Too bad," said the woman with a little shake of her head. "My daughter there, she is a widow too." She inclined her head toward a girl huddled in a back corner, a little slip of a thing who looked only nine or ten but who claimed to be thirteen when Amy asked her age. The little girl's harsh white sari stood out in bold contrast to the vivid colors that the other women wore, the love of every Indian woman's heart. But the most obvious difference about her was that she wore no jewels. Curses of widowhood.

"Yes, we married her to the old man down the street because he took a fancy to her and was willing to give us a large sum for her. But they were married only a year before he died. And now—well, of course she would have died at his burial if the British government had not made that against the law. But which is worse, to die right away, or to die slowly, living out a long life of widowhood?"

There were murmurs of agreement from the other women and then the silence of contemplation. Widowhood was a curse. What hope was there for a woman in the next life if she were not married? They had laughed at their young sister's joke about the men, but widowhood was a stark reality. Anyone who saw a widow in the daylight considered himself cursed too, so widows, even though they may have been only children when their husbands died, were often kept hidden away in inner rooms for the rest of their lives.

Amy's mind burned as it did every time she saw a widow, and even more when it was a child widow. "This was not her fault!" her mind cried. "Did you expect an old man to outlive a vivacious little girl? You treat her as if she killed him herself!" But she dare not say anything, or she would offend. These women didn't mean to be heartless; they just knew no other custom. This was the way their lives were. Only Jesus could change them. Amy threw a grateful glance at Ponnammal, living proof that Jesus could change a woman's heart.

Another woman broke the silence. "I suppose you are a widow too?" she asked, eyeing Amy.

"No," Amy replied. "I never married."

"Never married?"

"Never married!"

It was unheard of in India. No man or woman ever reached such an age as Amy had obviously reached without marrying *someone*.

"You mean you are married to a god," one woman interpreted.

"No," Amy answered hastily, "I am not married in any way. I did not marry so I can do the work of my God more easily. My work is to tell His great story of salvation to you."

With that introduction, Amy launched into a fresh explanation of the coming of the great God, Jesus Christ, of His salvation from sin, and of His promise for a home in heaven. But once again the women only stared at them. And one said, "We let our husbands study the religion. We simply take care of the house. It is growing late."

It wasn't, but Amy said, "Yes, we must be on our way."

"Yes, too bad. Come again!"

"Yes, come again!" Polite but insincere voices followed them.

The two ladies had time to enter one last house before departing. Here they found a sight similar to the one they had left, except that this time a baby was crying and children played noisily. In the dim light Amy could see that two or three of the women had white ashes smeared on their foreheads, a sure sign that they worshiped Siva, one of the three main Hindu gods.

When she saw some young girls there, Amy asked tentatively, "Can anyone here read?"

"Read?" The women laughed as if they had heard the best of jokes. "No. No one here can read."

"If you would send us these girls just a few hours a week, we could teach them." Teaching reading was one of the best opportunities to teach the gospel.

"Now why would we want to do that?" An older woman scoffed. "No woman in India learns to read except the servants of the gods. They have a reason to." Temple women, who were "married to the god," were generally regarded as the greatest of religious servants. But they learned to read just so they could quote religious poetry by the hundreds of stanzas—poetry that was unrepeatable in any other language.

"We do not need to be able to read in order to care for the babies and feed the cows and spank the children. You speak to us if you like, but let the men do the reading."

Amy spent an hour there telling the women about the love of Jesus. Bulls and cows wandered through the hut as she spoke, and the babies distracted her some, but she saw that the women really seemed to be paying attention. With joy she noticed that one old lady couldn't take her eyes off her as she spoke. "She is close to Jesus," Amy thought.

But suddenly the woman interrupted Amy's story and pointed to her hair. "Why don't you put oil in your hair?" she demanded. Amy was speechless.

"Yes," said another lady. "I was wondering that too." She stroked her own oil-laden tresses.

And then the other ladies joined in. "Can you not afford it?"

"Is it not your custom?"

"Castor oil is wonderful in the hair."

Amy heaved her shoulders helplessly. Could it possibly be that she had been speaking for a whole hour and these women hadn't heard a word she had said?

Amy and Ponnammal sang, but they left when the women seemed to be growing restless. "Come back again!" their hostesses called out jovially.

Meal time was approaching; so Amy and Ponnammal didn't try to enter any more homes. They knew that just the glance of a white woman on their food would make these caste-conscious people feel that they had to throw their whole dinner away and start their cooking all over again with fresh food. Or, if there was none, they would go hungry. And then they would be in no mood to listen to the gospel. So the two ladies headed back toward the bandy.

As usual on their visits in villages, little children followed them in the streets, children who were not too afraid of what their parents would say if it was discovered they had talked with the Christians. For a few moments they listened to the story of Jesus.

Some of the children seemed to be interested; it was different from anything they had ever heard before. As the night drew near, Amy promised, "We will come back and tell you more another day." She pulled her tired muscles into the bandy for the jolting ride home.

The two women rode in silence for some minutes as Amy searched for words to describe her feelings. Then she said, "Sometimes I think that the children listen better than most of the women do. So many of their minds are so . . . so *small*."

"The Indian woman's mind is small because her world is small," Ponnammal answered slowly. "Her whole life revolves around her family and the other women in one little village." She gestured back to the row upon row of drab brown huts they had left behind. "Her husband orders her not to think of religion or philosophy—he tells her to rub ashes on her forehead, and she does it. The average Indian woman thinks no higher thoughts than the gossip she hears around the village well. You ask most women about the next life, and they will smile and shrug. It is too far away."

"But what about you, Ponnammal? You heard and trusted. And what about the others in the Starry Cluster? All of you love the Lord so much that you even gave up your jewels for Him."

"Ah, yes." Ponnammal nodded wisely. "Sometimes, even to the foolish, the Lord bends down and opens the ears, opens the eyes. There is still hope, even for the smallest of women's minds."

Chapter Fourteen
Debates and Devils

Another day Amy and Ponnammal once again got into a bandy and rode to a village to find some women to tell the good news to, this time to a higher-caste village. They left the bandy just outside the village and got out to walk among the houses.

"Wait." An old man stopped them politely, but not quite sure that they should continue on their way. "What books do you have there?"

Amy felt a little impatient. After all, if the men wanted to hear the truth, there were many meetings and preachings they could attend. The women were the ones who were shut up in the houses; they were her mission field. But she collected herself and answered him politely. "This is a Bible, my holy Book. And these are books of Tamil poetry."

The man was visibly surprised. "Tamil poetry?" He closed his eyes and began quoting stanza upon stanza of the poems. When they heard him, some other old men came round, eyeing Amy suspiciously.

"Do you, a white woman, like this poetry?" the old man asked abruptly.

"I certainly do," Amy answered stoutly. "It's beautiful, and I wish I could understand the language and beauty of it even better than I do."

Suddenly the disposition of the whole group changed. The men warmed to the conversation and with vigor began discussing philosophical and religious issues with Amy and Ponnammal. They began to talk in such lofty terms that Amy couldn't understand most of what they were saying.

"Do you believe in God?" she finally asked.

"Yes, one god."

"But then why do you worship so many different idols?"

The men smiled as if they were talking to a child. "We believe in one god, but one who manifests himself in many different forms. Our Krishna, your Jesus, the Mohammed that the Moslems worship—all are manifestations of the same god. And the statues that you say we worship are but representations of god. We do not worship the statues, but what they represent. The divine god is in everything."

"But you yourselves know that the ignorant people really do worship those idols," Ponnammal interjected. "They think that those idols really *are* gods!"

The first man flicked his hand in a gesture of contempt. "Oh, the masses. They cannot understand our high thoughts about our god. They have to have their own little beliefs. That is how they have to worship because they can understand nothing else."

"That is the beauty of Hinduism," another man added. "Anyone, high or low, can worship, and each can make of the religion what he sees fit. He can worship one god, or he can worship thousands. Or if he believes that Brahman, Vishnu, and Siva are the holy triad, then he can decide which of those he believes is most powerful and worship him. Is it not a beautiful religion? And it has endured much longer than your Christianity."

Amy threw a despairing glance to Ponnammal. But one man was leafing through the Bible. "What sort of book is this?" he asked.

"It is my holy Book." Amy knew that the Hindus had great respect for any book that anyone called holy.

The man came upon I John 5:11-12. " 'God hath given to us eternal life, and this life is in his Son. He that hath the Son hath life; and he that hath not the Son of God hath not life.' What does this mean?"

Amy stopped and prayed quickly for wisdom. "The Son is Jesus," she began, "and if He indwells a person, then that person can live forever."

The men paused in thought.

"I believe that," said one.

"Yes, so do I," said another.

Amy could hardly contain her excitement. But as she watched the men's faces, she began to realize what they meant. And then they went on. "The eternal god indwells every person, just as he indwells everything, even the rocks. And as we are born again and again and finally are swallowed up in the essence of God, that is how we live forever." The men smiled and nodded and seemed satisfied.

Then they talked on and on, presenting arguments for Hinduism that began to boggle Amy's western mind. "We need to get to the women," she kept thinking. Finally she said, "Sirs, we have come here to talk to the women about religion; so—"

One younger man laughed. "The women! Can they even understand what you tell them?"

As Amy was about to make a stout defense of her work, an old man interrupted her. "Young man, you have much to learn, I see. It is because you are not yet married." The others laughed as the old man continued. "The women may say they are nothing when it comes to religion. But in all practicality, they are its heart. If men want even to listen to the talk of another religion and the women are not in favor of it, they will badger them mercilessly or humiliate them publicly until they are ashamed to be seen entertaining such ideas. The men may be the head of our religion, but the women are its heart."

As Amy was about to leave, she stopped to ask the men if they would be willing to set up a meeting with Mr. Walker.

"Certainly, certainly," one answered. "Hinduism can incorporate any other belief into itself. It—it swallows them up. It is truly a versatile religion."

Amy smiled weakly, but Ponnammal spoke. "Sahib," she addressed one of the men respectfully, "have you ever sinned?"

The man paused while he contemplated this question. "Some of our great men have had a deep sense of sin," he began. "They have gone through grievous tortures and long vigils to cleanse themselves of it in hopes, of course, of becoming one with god sooner. Now, I, on the other hand, have no great sense of sin. I have done things that you may regard as sin. But to me they are just practicalities of life.

Occasionally, I have to overcharge my customers to put enough bread on the table. Sometimes, perhaps I beat my wife a little too hard because she has burnt my dinner. But no, I have not committed any real sins." He stopped as if a thought had suddenly occurred to him. "I have never committed the sin for which there is no pardon."

Amy's curiosity overcame her. "What is that?" she asked.

"I have never killed a sacred cow."

"Oh, no," the men murmured. And another one added, "Other acts may be sins or may not be sins. But the killing of the sacred cow will assure a man that he will suffer in the next life."

Ponnammal started to make a reply to that, but Amy interrupted. "Mr. Walker will be glad to talk to you more on this matter," she said. And she motioned to Ponnammal to follow her to the village.

"I'm not sure that it was worth our time to talk with them any more," Amy explained. "They are intelligent, but they are not very wise."

As they entered the village, Amy noticed a man twisting the tail of a bony, half-dead ox, whose back was loaded with a far greater weight than it could carry. He twisted the tail again and again until the ox bellowed in pain.

Amy's animal-loving heart was filled with horror. "Stop! Why are you doing that?" she cried.

"He will not move, this lazy beast," the man grunted between clenched teeth.

"B-but this is one of your sacred beasts! How can you commit such a sin?"

The man stopped his torture to eye Amy. "Listen, white woman," he said. "I am not killing the ox. *That* would be a sin. I am only teaching it to mind me. You had best be on your way."

Amy quickly stepped out of the man's way, but she was still filled with indignation as she tried to shut out the sounds of the bellowing ox. When she was out of earshot, she said to Ponnammal, "Do the Hindus often practice such inconsistencies?"

"Oh, yes," came the reply. "This religion is full of them."

The houses in the little village they entered were noticeably nicer than the huts they had canvassed the day before. Wide porches extended right through the houses to airy courtyards behind. But these people were so conscious of their caste that they would not let a white woman enter their houses. Amy and Ponnammal had to stand outside and sing, hoping a crowd would gather.

As the sun beat down hotter and hotter, Amy began to feel faint. But she continued to try to sing and talk and read from her own sacred Book.

People came and went. They gathered to see if what was being said was of any interest to them, and they left when something else interested them more. Only a few stayed long enough to understand anything Amy and Ponnammal were trying to tell them. Sometimes women interrupted them with off-the-subject questions about their caste or their family. Once a man entered the group and tried to draw the women away with what he considered were logical stumpers about the Christian religion. Amy tried to keep to the subject of Jesus while still being polite.

All along there were always the sounds of cows lowing and donkeys braying, children yelling and babies crying. Finally a dog came yelping down the street, stones flying around it. A pack of little boys ran at full tilt after it, yelling and screaming. That was enough to break up the group and send each woman running to her respective door, where she stood watching the two missionary women, who finally decided it was time to go home. Back down the road they plodded.

A group of teen-age boys had sat on a porch the whole time, watching the women. "Who will fall into the pit of the Christian way?" one sneered. The women didn't turn to look as they continued on their way.

Amy and Ponnammal got back in the bandy and began the two-hour ride back to the mission compound. But suddenly they were startled by the noise of a stampede of people tearing along the streets, yelling and screaming, banging on drums. As it came closer, they saw the purpose for the stampede—huge and gaudy idols were held aloft on platforms by dozens of the throng. Amidst all the uproar Amy could make out some chants and prayers being made to these idols. The people thronged the road and kept the bandy from going any farther.

"We can't just sit here!" Amy whispered feverishly to Ponnammal. "Sing!"

At the top of their lungs the two women sang, "Victory to Jesus' Name! Victory!" Miraculously, a few people were actually able to hear them, and got a chance, for a few moments at least, to hear of Jesus.

Darkness was falling. Amy watched as the heathen people lit torches and danced around a huge bush, hair streaming, bright colors flashing in the flickering lights, yelling prayers and eulogies to their idols, beating their drums harder, faster, louder. As the bandy was able to move farther and farther away from the riot, she could finally look down on it from a distance. The sight reminded her of hell.

They continued on in silence for a while. Then Ponnammal said, "Those are the masses that one old man said need to practice their religion that way because that is the only thing they understand."

Amy nodded wordlessly. Then she added thoughtfully, "I can't get out of my mind something one man said—that Hinduism can swallow up any other religion. It reminded me of the cows in Pharaoh's dream. It can keep on swallowing them up and swallowing them up. But it will still be just as lean as before."

Chapter Fifteen
A Festival and a Funeral

"I have to keep telling myself that this is a golden opportunity," Amy sighed as she put on her sari and got ready to leave. "I absolutely *hate* these festivals."

"But so many people are all gathered together," Ponnammal encouraged her. "All with plenty of free time to listen to our good news."

"That's what I have to keep telling myself. My, but the Indian people do love a function! Only 365 days in the year, and 200 of them are dedicated to some festival or other."

There in the temple courtyard were hundreds and thousands of Hindus all gathered for the festival to one of their gods, all engaged in the festival's main attraction—the killing of goats for the sacrifices. Hundreds of goatskins hung from trees. Amy turned to avoid the sight but only saw men in the act of slicing goats' necks. The poor little creatures' bodies kicked and writhed even after their heads had been severed. She felt sick.

"I thought we were coming late enough to avoid this part," she said, holding her head.

"I did too," Ponnammal answered ruefully. "I am sorry."

Finally they found a tree under which they could rest. There were no leaves, but at least the trunk provided some shade. A little boy nearby was playing with one of the goats' heads. Amy turned away again.

The two women sang and managed to get a small group of women around them so that they could tell them about Jesus. This group had to leave, and another came. Then another and another. With each they managed to plant a few seeds of the gospel.

But no group had time to listen for long. There were goats to kill and dinners to eat and games to play and pots to buy.

All the vendors had taken advantage of the festival, Amy could see. Their makeshift shops sat crunched up against each other in the courtyard. The two women left the shade of the tree and moved from booth to booth, hoping to find another place to stop to talk about Jesus.

All through the courtyard, the vendors' booths jammed between and around them, stood small idols and shrines. Amy watched as a devout worshiper would rise from groveling in the dust before his god and move two steps to the left to begin haggling in angry tones over the price of a clay pot.

"Buy my wares! Buy my wares!" the languid sing-song chant came at them from all directions. One toothy young boy held up a large blue pot while a toothless old man shoved a scarlet sari under Amy's nose. A woman covered with jewels draped herself over pillows and dropped necklaces made of colored glass from one hand to the other, trying to entice

someone to buy. A girl carrying a plate strolled from booth to booth to sell cakes that smelled inviting but were covered with flies. Rugs splashed with rainbows of color decorated a booth directly behind a blind beggar holding out a broken cup.

Beggars, thieves, snake charmers, jeweled merchants, all moved about among the booths and the cows—bony and forlorn, trying half-heartedly to swat the flies that persisted in settling on their backs. Amy fanned herself, but the heat and the stench and the flies were almost overpowering.

A cake seller finally offered them a bit of shade, and they had opportunities to witness and sell some of the Gospels they carried. When the cake-woman found that they were taking business that she felt rightfully belonged to her, they bought some of her cakes and she was satisfied.

Amy and Ponnammal moved on, stepping carefully through the courtyard, trying their best to avoid the unidentified debris underfoot. Soon they found an empty stall where they were once again able to rest and attract a few listeners. But it wasn't long before Amy began to feel faint again. "Ponnammal, I'm so hot and thirsty. I'm afraid I'm going to be sick."

"If only we had something to drink, you would be all right. But we don't have any money to buy anything."

"We spent it all on those impossible cakes," Amy moaned.

An enterprising young buttermilk seller, obviously seeing the women's thirst, approached them with a gleam in his eye. He had already poured a cup of buttermilk by the time he reached their stall.

Amy licked her parched lips. "But we don't have any money," she admitted with great regret.

"Oh." And he poured it back. "Still, you are obviously very thirsty. And giving to the poor is a good deed that will serve me well in the next life. So even though I am poor. . . ." And he began to pour again.

Amy hesitated. She hated to take the buttermilk from a poor man, but she was *so* thirsty.

The bookseller in the next stall saw their plight. "Here," he called. And he threw the young man a coin. Amy and Ponnammal smiled at him gratefully as they each downed a big cup of buttermilk.

"Let me give you some of our books to pay for the milk you bought us," Amy urged.

The man smiled and shrugged. He didn't need the books, didn't care about them in the least. The merit he had earned by his good deed would go unrewarded.

After resting, the two women left their stall and walked on to the steps of the temple. This gorgeously decorated building, with its carved figures and intricate filigree work, was the ultimate destination of all the worshipers—ardent and reverent or careless and frivolous. Here they carried the bodies of the goats they had slaughtered or pulled bucking and kicking live ones to slay right before the idol in the dimly lit depths of this devil-hole.

The crowd swept up the steps with such force and abandon that Amy and Ponnammal were carried in before they even knew what was happening. On through the depths of the inner shrine and then to an enclosed temple courtyard they were swept. They found that the women here were talking and laughing just as had the ones outside.

But the women stopped short at the sight of Amy. Not that they had never before seen a white woman. But they knew that no white person was allowed inside their sacred temple. Because of the unusual circumstances, Amy had a greater opportunity than ever to witness. When the night drew near and they felt they had done all they could, the two missionaries finally departed.

It wasn't many days later that Amy was able to witness another sight that few white women had ever seen. She and Ponnammal arrived in a village to find the death-drums beating. A shiver ran up Amy's spine as she realized what it meant.

The women of the village gathered around the two visitors in eager excitement. "He was a great man! There will be a tremendous ceremony for him!" And they clapped their hands and dispersed to their houses as the procession of men marched down the street to bathe in the river before the funeral ceremony took place.

Before long the two ladies found the house of the dead man. Garlands were being hung over the door, servants were rushing about to prepare food, and women were laughing and talking with the same air of excitement they had expressed earlier. This was an event, and the man was no relation of theirs. So long as the tragedy didn't touch them, it was a great show. And the Indian people dearly loved a show of any kind.

Amy stood at a safe distance so as to not defile the caste-conscious Hindus. As she watched the proceedings, she heard a loud wail rise from within the house. And again, and again. It was the dead man's family. But the women outside continued to laugh and talk as if they hadn't heard the wailing at all.

When one of the women noticed Amy and Ponnammal, she invited them to come join the group and see the show. "It does not matter!" she exclaimed jovially when Amy expressed surprise. "We are all defiled anyway. It is a funeral! We will wash later. Look! They are preparing the sacrifice for the Brahmins to offer."

With delight Amy squeezed in next to the women that she ordinarily was not allowed to touch. She tried to take advantage of the opportunity to talk with them about what lies beyond the grave, but there were too many sights to see. It all reminded Amy of the festival.

Finally the body of the dead man was carried out. There he lay, thin and worn, still bearing the marks of his god on his forehead. But the women confided in Amy and Ponnammal that he had always been uncertain about eternity. "He died not knowing what lay on the other side," they told them.

For one part of the ceremony the women were ordered inside. Quiet and awed now, they listened to the rise and fall of the sing-song chant that the Brahmin priest uttered over the dead man's body. But even during this proceeding, the wail of the bereaved family still rose and fell in the inner chambers of the house.

When the women were allowed back out, they found the men preparing rice balls and torches for the dead man to take with him into the land of the spirits of the dead. He would be hungry, surely. He would need light in that dark place. And all the little grandchildren marched around his body with candles, looking awed by the ceremony they were taking part in.

Then the dead man's widow stumbled out of the house, held up by two other women. "He has left me desolate!" she wailed. "Is he truly dead? Oh, oh, come back to me. Speak to me! Am I to suffer the horrors of widowhood? Are you truly dead? Is there no way I can reach you?" She wailed again, a shuddering cry, and collapsed in a heap on the ground. The other family members sat in a circle around the body and swayed back and forth in agony, holding each other or holding themselves. Some even tore their hair. "Is he really gone to the land of the spirits of the dead? Will he never return? Oh, speak one last time!"

Amy watched in horror. "These are the ones," she thought, "that Paul was referring to when he spoke of 'others who have no hope.' " She realized that she couldn't speak to the family members now, with the agony they were suffering. And later, after the man's body had been burned on his funeral pyre and the family returned from their purification bathing in the river, they did not want to have anything to do with her.

Later that night Amy mused once again over the people that she loved and wanted to reach for Jesus. "You know, Ponnammal," she said thoughtfully, "I often used to read books about missionaries who journeyed to a foreign country and found that the heathen there had just been praying to know the truth. When the missionary brought the gospel, they were more than ready to receive it. I find that real life doesn't often work that way."

Chapter Sixteen
The Living God

Little did Amy Carmichael know, that one ten-year-old girl in a remote Indian village was praying to know the truth.

Arulai had a mean temper. She would get angry at her friends and hit them, making them afraid to play with her. "Why does this happen?" Arulai asked over and over. "I want to be good, but my temper takes over my whole body." She begged her father to tell her. "Is Siva the greatest god? I rub his ashes on my forehead every morning. But I have prayed to him again and again, and he has not changed my temper."

"Child, I know of no god that can make a bad disposition into a good one," Arulai's father answered. "That is something you must do yourself."

And yet Arulai felt sure that if she could only find the one God that is the greatest of all gods, He would be the one that could help her. Surely if there were a God that was all-powerful, then He could do that. One more time she tried. "O heavenly Siva," she cried, "hear me, I pray, and change my disposition!

Help the other children to love me! Hear me, Siva! Hear me!"

When Siva did not answer, she tried praying to Brahma, to Vishnu, and even to other lesser gods, hoping that someone had made a mistake and that one of them really was the greatest. But it became obvious to her that none of them were. Her temper didn't change a bit.

"What good does it do to pray to any god," she finally asked herself, "if he is not the greatest God of all? I want to worship Him. But alas! I do not know who He is!" And the girl ran into a field where she threw herself on the ground and cried, "O greatest of all the gods, hear me, even though I do not know who You are! Hear me, I pray, and show Yourself to me!"

But no answer came. Finally she rose, brushed herself off, and went home, sighing heavily with sadness.

A great blow came to Arulai when her baby brother, whom she had cared for and loved dearly, died suddenly. "Where is he now?" she begged of her mother. "I want to be able to picture him somewhere."

"All I know, child," her mother answered wearily, "is that he is in the land of the spirits of the dead."

Arulai clinched her eyes shut and tried to imagine her little brother in that dismal land, floating around among all those other spirits of the dead, not knowing anyone, crying for his beloved sister. The God of gods was great, she was sure. But was He really good, to do such a thing to a little baby boy?

Still, something inside her pulled at her heart to try to find that greatest God. She planned special places and times to pray to Him, even though she still did not know His name.

One day as Arulai set out to the well to draw water, she didn't happen to be thinking about God. She was just thinking about getting the water and getting home on time. But there, near the well, she saw an Indian man and some foreigners, with a few people gathered around them. Arulai glanced at them out of curiosity—she had never seen foreigners before. She was moving in the direction of home, though, when these words that the Indian man spoke burned their way into her heart: *"There is a living God! There is a living God! I was a lion, and He turned me into a lamb!"*

Arulai stopped short. That was it! That was what she had been waiting months and months to hear! If only she had time to stay and find out the name of this living God—but she had to hurry home or face a beating from her mother.

Why, if there were one living God, that meant that Siva was a dead god. She determined not to rub his ashes on her forehead anymore.

That night she lay wide awake thinking of the living God and praying to Him. She prayed especially that He would send those foreigners to her village again so that she could find out about Him.

And the next day they were there again, around the well, preaching and talking. Arulai only glanced at the Indian women in the group. But she stopped and studied the foreigners. There were three of them— an older couple, and one younger *ammal,* or woman, wearing a sari. "The older couple looks as if they must be married," Arulai mused. "But I don't see how they could be when they seem to be so devoted to their God. Maybe they were married before they came to know this God; so they were not able to separate themselves from each other. They must be embarrassed by it.

"I don't understand, either, how they could seem so happy. People who are devoted to a god are always sad. But anyway, I think I like the looks of that younger *ammal*. She is wearing a sari; so I think I will go to her. She can explain all about the living God to me and then I can worship Him. . . ."

It suddenly occurred to Arulai that her family would not like for her to be worshiping a god other than Siva, even though he was dead. That meant that if she were to worship the living God, she would have great difficulties. "But I know," she whispered to herself confidently, "that someday the living God will bring me to this *ammal* in the sari, and I will be her daughter, and when I learn all about Him, I will go around as she does now and tell others about Him."

Although she wasn't able to talk to the foreign woman in the sari yet, Arulai listened closely to the words that these people spoke about the living God. She went to the meeting that they had later, where several other children were gathered. On her way home, Arulai had doubts about the living God. Did He, after all, really exist? Or had her hopes imagined that He could be real? She decided on a test, to see if He really was alive. "I will ask Him three things," she said. "If He grants me two of them, I will believe that He is the living God."

There on the doorstep she saw her mother standing with a broom in her hand, waiting to punish her.

"Living God," Arulai prayed, "my first request is that You keep my mother from punishing me!"

But Arulai's mother grabbed her by the arm and swatted her again and again. "You have been listening to those low-caste people!" she cried. "You are a disgrace to our family! You must be punished for that!"

Arulai felt miserable. She didn't mind the punishment half so much as she worried over the thought that the living God had not been able to answer her prayer.

But the next day she went to hear the foreigners again. Amidst the group of children she sat, eager to learn more about this new God. Suddenly she heard the question, "Has anyone been punished for coming to hear about Jesus Lord?" Arulai was embarrassed to answer, but another child, who knew of her trouble, pointed her out. "If you are punished," the woman said, "call upon the name of Jesus Lord and look to Him in your heart, and He will give you strength to face the trouble."

When Arulai left the meeting that day, she murmured the name *Jesus Lord* to herself over and over. Why, this was the name of the living God! She skipped along the path, so happy was she to know it at last. And as she skipped, she thought of her test. There was a tamarind tree, heavy with sweet fruit, but none was on the ground around it. The law in India said that you must not steal fruit from the tree, but if it falls to the ground, it is yours. So Arulai prayed, "Jesus Lord, living God, make the fruit fall at my feet." Suddenly, a pod fell.

The little Indian girl picked up the pod with a feeling of awe, sure that Jesus Lord had done this for her. Now there was only one more prayer—if He were to answer this one, she would be sure that He was indeed the greatest of all the gods.

As she neared her house, Arulai's heart beat with fear. "Jesus Lord, do not let my mother punish me," she prayed. "Show me that You are the living God."

There was her mother at the doorstep, but she did not have the broom in her hand. All she said was, "Come in, child. I thought you were lost."

That settled it. Jesus Lord was the living God, the greatest of all the gods.

Chapter Seventeen
The *Ammal* in the Sari

Every day Arulai prayed to her living God. She sensed His presence around her everywhere she went, and it gave her great comfort. But one thing she continued to pray. "Jesus Lord, take me to the *ammal* in the sari soon, if You please. I want so much to learn about You from her." Arulai didn't have any idea where or how far away the *ammal* in the sari lived, but that didn't bother her a bit. She didn't even stop to worry that in all her life she had never left her little village. She knew that nothing was too hard for the living God.

"What will we do with this child?" Arulai's father complained. "She will not worship Siva as she should. She is bewitched with the worship of that Jesus Lord. Those Christians have bewitched her."

"Do you recall that my brother is a Christian?" her mother answered. "And he does not let his belief get in the way of his everyday life as Arulai is doing. Let us send her to his village to live with him for a while. That will knock some sense into her head."

So Arulai walked a day's journey to her uncle's village. Her uncle claimed to be a Christian, but his way of living confused her. He seemed to still fit in so well with the Hindu life. Slowly she began doing as he did. She tried not to let the Hindu prayers, practices, and celebrations bother her.

One day Arulai's uncle told her that within a year her father was going to make her get married, to be sure that she would not continue in her Christian beliefs.

"O living God!" she sobbed that night in her bed. "Living God, I do not want to be a heathen the rest of my life. I do not want to marry a heathen. I want to go to the *ammal* in the sari. Please, please take me there before my father comes back to get me."

One day an older girl came up to Arulai. "Do you want to learn about the true God?" she asked.

"Yes, I do. I want to very much."

"Do you love Him?"

"Yes, with all my heart I do."

"Where did you first hear about Him?"

"In my village," Arulai answered. "Some Indian women and some foreigners were telling about Him."

"One of those Indian women is my mother," the older girl said. "I know all of them. They have been gone, but they will be back in two days. They live just over in the next village. Their house is right next to the Christian temple."

In the next village! Arulai's heart leaped for joy. The living God had heard her prayer! And they would be back in two days! She could hardly wait—her heart pounded out the seconds as she returned to her uncle's house to dream of finally getting to see the *ammal* in the sari again.

Early Sunday morning Arulai set out for the neighboring village, eagerly anticipating the meeting with her special *ammal.* But as she trudged down the sandy path, a dismal thought came to her. "Jesus Lord, I have no offering to give You! I dare not go into Your temple without something to lay before You. I always gave offerings to those dead gods; now how much more important is it to give an offering to the living God! Whatever will I do?"

Even as she spoke these words, Arulai glanced down and saw a copper coin in her path. She wasn't surprised. This was something that the living God could do easily. But she was relieved and grateful. "Thank You, Jesus Lord," she whispered. "Now I do not need to be afraid to enter Your temple."

Arulai entered the church quietly, sitting near the back of the group of children and older people who were gathered there. She listened to a man preach about sin and punishment and God's love and salvation. The little Indian girl didn't understand much of it, but she listened to every word he said. When the offering plate was passed, she gratefully dropped in her copper coin.

Later Arulai finally got her chance to talk to the *ammal* in the sari. So many questions she had! Mainly she wanted to know where her little brother had gone when he died. Amy answered these questions, but she knew that what Arulai needed to hear most was the way of salvation. Arulai needed to hear about Jesus.

Slowly and carefully Amy explained the story of Jesus Lord and who He really is. In rapt attention the little girl listened to this new and wonderful story of the true God who became a man because of His great love.

"You mean they killed Him?" she asked.

"Yes, they killed Him because they hated Him. But that was the way He brought us salvation. And then He rose again from the dead after three days. He overcame sin and death, and when we become His, He gives us the power to overcome sin and death."

After Arulai accepted Christ as her Saviour, she wanted to know more and more about what being a Christian really meant. At every opportunity she ran from her uncle's village to the neighboring village to ask a new question that had come to her mind or just to hear more stories about Jesus Lord and His great love.

But one day when she came to visit Amy, she said, "My uncle has told me that my parents want me back in their village for four days. Just four days, and then I will be back."

Amy's heart sank. She tried to listen as she heard the little girl describing with pleasure all the wonderful things about her new Lord that she would tell her family. But even as she listened, Amy feared for Arulai's life. This had happened before. An Indian became a Christian, and then, mysteriously, he was never heard from again. Or he was discovered dead— by "accident." Or, worst of all, when he was seen again, he was a totally different person—no vitality, no personality. Just a puppet who would parrot back the Hindu beliefs that others around him spoke. The stories of the tortures that these Christians underwent to make them come to this point had struck horror to her heart.

As Arulai spoke glowingly of the gospel and how happy these four days would be for her, Amy tried to smile. But she still felt that sinking feeling in her heart. She feared that she would never see Arulai again.

And that was exactly what the family planned. They had heard of Arulai's renewed interest in Christianity, and they had no intention of letting her go back. They were planning to do everything they could to "encourage" her in the Hindu way.

Amy prayed desperately as days and weeks passed with no news. But when news finally did come, it wasn't good. Arulai was obeying, rubbing Siva's ashes on her forehead again. Soon, it was said, she would be married.

Amy, the Walkers, and all the Starry Cluster continued to pray for Arulai. They knew how hard it must be for such a young girl to stand up for the Lord when she knew so little of the strength and comfort He could give in such a time. They didn't doubt that in her heart Arulai still loved Him. Finally Amy felt led to send a messenger to Arulai's parents to ask if she could come back to learn, even for a short time.

At first Arulai's father refused with anger. But her mother said, "Let her go just to see the *ammal*. Maybe that will break the spell, and she will not be bewitched anymore." And so he consented at last. "But only for a day! Bring her back immediately."

In spite of those last words, Arulai's heart leaped with joy. If her living God could move her father's heart to let her go, she was sure that somehow she would be able to stay.

When Arulai reached Amy's village, she ran into the house. But when she fell into the arms of the *ammal* that she loved, she collapsed with a burning fever. She had become seriously ill while being persecuted at her father's house.

The Lord worked even through this terrible illness. Arulai was so sick that she couldn't leave the home of the Christians just yet. They had to keep her for several weeks and nurse her back to health. For a time she hovered between life and death. Finally, when she was well, her parents were grateful enough to let her live with her uncle once again and visit the missionaries. Arulai grew in her faith daily.

But one day her father came for her. The little girl ran into another room to pray. "My Lord Jesus, do not let him take me away," she begged. And her Lord gave her a promise from His Word that He would keep her safe.

With great peace Arulai came out to face her father. She kissed him and greeted him kindly. "My God has promised me that He will bring me back here no matter what happens," she announced joyfully.

Arulai's father was stunned. Although he did not want to speak, he seemed forced to say, "I cannot do anything against your powerful God!" When he reached out his arm to grab her, it fell limp at his side. "Read to me from your Book."

After she had read, he said, "Pray for me." She prayed. Then her father said weakly, "I will never take you away unless you want to go. I fear your supreme God."

Then he walked away, leaving a jubilant little Arulai in the care of her special *ammal*. There she stayed for many years, ministering to her people by telling them of the power and love of the living God.

Chapter Eighteen
Refuge for Children

"Refuge! Refuge, please!" The loud clapping outside continued until Mr. Walker, rubbing sleep from his eyes, stumbled groggily to open the door.

"Why, whatever is the matter, child?" Amy stood in the far doorway gazing at the wild-eyed teen-age girl that fell before them.

"I was sleeping in my house with my family." Her words seemed to tumble over each other. "And a voice inside of me said 'Go'; so I came here. I come here because I do not want the life that my family lives."

The sixteen-year-old girl, who became known as Jewel of Victory, told the missionaries her whole story when they brought her in and set her at a table. "My family does not know or care about the Christian Way," she explained, "but they sent me to a mission school simply to give me an education. They had no fears that I would follow the Way, because in sixty years only two people ever have. But I heard about Jesus at that mission school. I grew to love Him. My brother still rubbed Siva's ashes on my head, but I rubbed them off in secret.

"Then my family found out about my new beliefs. They were angry. My father lit a bonfire that leaped up into the heavens. He said, 'You follow this Jesus Way, and you will be part of this bonfire.' And I believed him, Missie, because I have known other people who have died for their beliefs. Then last night it seemed a voice told me to go, and I came here. Do you suppose it was the voice of Jesus?"

Jewel of Victory stayed on with the missionaries. But not without troubles: her family was determined to get her back. They didn't want the shame of having to admit that one of their caste had accepted Jesus as Saviour.

"But she is of age!" Amy explained loudly to the people who came almost every day. "She is free to make this decision for herself." Still they threatened to invade in the middle of the night, even to kill Jewel of Victory if they had to.

The girl was preserved, but the family burned down the mission school. In spite of all this, though, news of Jewel of Victory's acceptance of this new, strange God spread through other villages. Within six months another teen-age girl was banging on the mission house door, crying, "Refuge! Refuge!" Jewel of Life, as she was later named, also accepted the Lord as her Saviour and joined the band of missionaries that spring of 1899.

Even more unusual, though, was the coming of little Preena two years later, in the spring of 1901. Amy could never have forseen that Preena's coming would help to open a door of horrors that Amy had never before imagined.

Preena was only seven years old when her father died. Women from the Hindu temple came to her mother, offering to take care of Preena for her and raise her for temple service. Preena's mother, who was poor now that her husband had died, decided to let these women take her daughter and "marry her to the god." Then Preena's entire life would be dedicated to service in the Hindu temple.

But even as the temple women took Preena away, something in the little girl's heart felt afraid of going with these strange women to a mysterious new life. She ran away back to her mother. When the women followed and threatened her, Preena's mother pushed her back into the women's arms. They carried her to the temple, where they planned to marry her to the god as soon as they could. While they were still outside, though, they tried a trick to scare Preena into obeying them. They saw one of Amy Carmichael's Indian Christian friends and cried, "There is the child-stealing woman! Run!" But even as Preena ran with the temple servants, she glanced back curiously to try to see the child-stealing woman.

Since Preena had tried to get back to her mother, the temple women punished her by branding her hands with a hot iron. Then Preena stayed in the dark temple for days, where she felt terribly afraid and alone. Finally she fell in front of the Hindu idol and prayed, "Let me die. Please let me die!" But even as she lay before it, a voice seemed to say within her, "Get up quickly. Go."

Because it was late at night, Preena was able to sneak out of the temple and run as fast as she could through the town. She didn't know where she was going, but she did know one thing. "I want to find that child-stealing woman," she thought. She wandered to another village, where she found a church, and there she stood for a while.

At last the Lord brought along another Christian Indian woman, named Servant of Jesus. She spoke to Preena and then took her to her own home. "I will take you back to your people," Servant of Jesus said.

"No!" insisted Preena. "I want to find the child-stealing woman. I want her to steal me away from that temple."

When Servant of Jesus realized that Preena was a temple child, she agreed that the temple was an evil place. But who was this child-stealing woman Preena was talking about? Servant of Jesus finally decided that it must be Amy Carmichael, who had helped Arulai escape from her Hindu home. So she took Preena to the mission, where Amy welcomed her with open arms.

But it wasn't long before temple women crowded around the mission. "Give the child back to us!" they cried. "She belongs to the temple!"

Amy knew that Preena was safe as long as she would not consent to go with the women. But the temple women seemed to have some kind of power over her, and as much as Preena wanted to stay at the mission, Amy was afraid that she would finally say yes.

Quickly Arulai took Preena away so she wouldn't have to face the women. The poor little seven-year-old was terribly afraid. "If I say no, they will beat me!" she sobbed. But soon she had enough courage to come back and say, "I won't! I won't!" Finally the temple women left.

Then Preena told Amy and the others the secrets of the temple that she knew about from her stay there. "The priests and worshipers do whatever they want to you," she explained. Amy and the other Christians recoiled in horror. "I knew it was an evil place," one of them whispered. "But they let no one know how completely evil it is. No one except the most devout 'worshipers,' that is."

"We have to find out if what Preena says is true," Amy said.

Ponnammal objected. "But you know that no one except worshipers can go into the temple."

"That doesn't matter," Amy replied. "Somehow, somehow we have to find the truth."

Chapter Nineteen
Searching for Temple Secrets

"Look," Amy said to Ponnammal. "Does my skin look dark enough for people to think I'm an Indian?" She held out one hand that had been laboriously stained with coffee.

"Why, whatever are you doing, Amma?" Ponnammal asked with a smile, using the Indian term of endearment that meant "mother."

"I have to find out if what Preena tells me about the horrors of the temple is true," Amy said. "And you know better than I do that in India you don't find out much by asking questions. People get suspicious of you. You can find out a lot more by just blending in with the crowd and listening to what people say. And I need to be able to get inside places that a white woman wouldn't be allowed to enter. I need to find answers *now*."

Ponnammal's face grew serious. "You will be taking quite a risk, Amma," she said. "But yes, your arm does look a proper shade of brown."

A while later Amy appeared before some of the others in her sari, holding out her coffee-stained arms.

"You look like a regular Indian woman, Amma!" Jewel of Life cried. "You could fit into any crowd."

Arulai studied her. "It is a good thing that you do not have blue eyes as some of the foreign missionaries do," she observed. "Someone would surely see then that you were not an Indian."

Amy laughed in agreement as she turned to leave the room. But she stopped for a moment, pondering what Arulai had said. *It is a good thing that you do not have blue eyes.* . . . A memory, an old, old memory began to move to the forefront of her mind— a memory of a little girl, only three years old, crying because her eyes were not blue . . . of that same little girl finally being convinced that Jesus had made her with brown eyes for a very special purpose, and that He knew what was right. Tears came to Amy's eyes, and she said, "Yes, Lord, You truly did know what was right all along. Thank You for showing me once again."

Later as Amy thought about God's ways in answering prayer, she wrote this poem:

> Just a tiny little child
>   Three years old,
> And a mother with a heart
>   All of gold.
> Often did that mother say,
> Jesus hears us when we pray,
> For He's never far away
>   And He always answers.
>
> Now, that tiny little child
>   Had brown eyes,
> And she wanted blue instead
>   Like blue skies.

For her mother's eyes were blue
Like forget-me-nots. She knew
All her mother said was true;
  Jesus always answered.

So she prayed for two blue eyes,
  Said "Good night,"
Went to sleep in deep content
  And delight.
Woke up early, climbed a chair
By a mirror. Where, O where
Could the blue eyes be? Not there;
  Jesus hadn't answered.

Hadn't answered her at all;
  Never more
Could she pray; her eyes were brown
  As before.
Did a little soft wind blow?
Came a whisper soft and low,
"Jesus answered. He said,'No';
  Isn't *No* an answer?"

Amy was determined to use her Indian disguise to penetrate the most horrid secrets of the Hindu religion. But it didn't prove to be as easy as she had hoped it would be.

For one thing, Amy wasn't able to devote all her time to the discovering of temple secrets. She was still witnessing with the Starry Cluster and still taking care of day-to-day problems that arose at the mission.

But as she and faithful Ponnammal traveled together, other problems arose that Amy hadn't anticipated. For one thing, even most Hindus didn't know what really went on behind the closed doors of the temple. But also the more "devout" worshipers, who observed and participated in the temple horrors, were wary of speaking of their religious practices. The British government controlled India at the time, and these Hindus knew that if the British discovered the truth, they would be punished and have to put an end to their evil practices.

Other missionaries scoffed at the idea that such things would be happening to little children. But Amy was still determined to prove the truth. For three long years she searched for proof.

The determined Irish lady grew discouraged, but she didn't give up. She and Ponnammal stood around village wells where women liked to gather to gossip. They stayed in an inn where priests and worshipers were gathered. They hid in barns and lofts.

Finally Amy and Ponnammal did find out the different ways that children were given over to temple service in the first place. Sometimes if the parents were suffering through a hard time they would say, "If the god will deliver me from this suffering, I will give my child to be married to him." Sometimes a man who felt he had too many daughters to provide for would give one to the god just to avoid having to take care of her. Sometimes a widow would do the same thing, because she simply didn't have the money to care for her child, and she thought that the child would be suitably cared for in the temple. Sometimes both parents would die, or for one reason or another they would abandon their baby. And the evil temple women were always on the lookout for pretty, intelligent girls.

"Just think," Amy thought to herself, "most of these horrible women were probably once beautiful little girls themselves. And some awful 'servants of the gods' stole them away to grow up in that terrible place. And this is how they turned out. This is what Preena would have been like twenty years from now."

After much practice at pretending to be an Indian woman, Amy took the final step. She ventured into the temple itself, walking past the priests that stood at the doors. Her steps echoed in the stone hallway. "This is quite different from that festival day," she thought. The temple was dark. "As dark as the pits of hell," she thought, shuddering. In one shrine stood the devilishly ugly idol, the one that these poverty-stricken people sacrificed their goods and their children to. Amy shuddered again. Then she saw the priest and the children, beautiful little girls just like Preena. Amy knew that what she had heard was true. Hardly anyone knew that these little girls were "married to the god" just so that they could live a life of unthinkable shame. But Amy knew now. Her world turned black as she realized the horrible truth and thought of all the children throughout India that needed to be rescued from this life.

Chapter Twenty
Rescue

"Sister Amy Carmichael," Mr. Walker began deliberately. Before he had gotten any further, giggles sounded all around the table from the girls seated there. "What was the meaning of that squirrel running across my breakfast?"

Amy felt like a child again. "Well, Brother Walker," she began, "while you were gone away on your speaking engagement, we allowed the squirrel to come to breakfast with us, and it didn't understand why it couldn't come to the table today. I tried to explain," she added feebly.

More giggles.

"But you obviously didn't teach it good table manners in my absence if it would go flying through the butter and upsetting the milk jug. Not to mention jumping all over my shoulders."

Giggles.

"But that was just because it was nervous. It did so want to make a good impression on you, Brother." Amy glanced around at the merry faces and suddenly felt a little more spunky. "Besides, Brother Walker, animals are God's creatures too, and if you don't like them, then perhaps there is something wrong with you."

"I do like them," Mr. Walker told her icily, "when they are where they belong. Squirrels belong in trees, not in butter dishes."

Later that day Amy told Preena and Arulai some of the animal escapades she had experienced as a little girl. "I used to think that animals were just as important as people," she said with a laugh. "It took me a long time to be convinced that they weren't going to go to heaven." She sighed. "It's still a little hard for me to believe."

After the little girls had gone to bed, Amy talked with Ponnammal. "I'm so glad to have children in the house," she said. "I had no idea how much I had missed their presence." She lay awake long hours that night thinking of the many children throughout southern India that were in danger of temple service. "Lord," she prayed, "please help me to be able to do something! It seems that every time we try to rescue a child, the doors slam in our faces."

Over two years had gone by since little Preena's coming. The mission work had moved to a new place, in Dohnavur. The total amount of land came to several acres, but they'd had to buy it in tiny pieces, because one man who owned a piece of land would leave one part of it to each son, who in turn would split up his piece of land and give part to each son. After several generations had gone by, one man might own just a few square feet of land! But he would jealously guard it, and if the Christians had built a building on land that they didn't own—even if it was just a little sliver—they could be taken to court. The process of buying had taken several months and lots of patience. But now the Lord was helping them to transform the mission site from the barren wilderness area that it had been to a lush, beautiful garden with plenty of room to rear children for Him. And Amy hadn't given up. She was still looking for them, still hopeful.

Amy had found some children in danger. But she hadn't been successful in getting any of them. "To dedicate my child to the gods would be eternal glory," the Hindus would say. "But to give her to you would be eternal disgrace. So why should I give her to you?" And one woman said, "If those wicked Christians offered me gold piled as high as this child's head, I would not give her to them."

Sometimes Amy spoke with beautiful little girls who were with their "adopted mothers"—the temple servants. "Do you want to see my wedding jewel?" an innocent child would ask. And she would pull out a lovely little gold ornament on a gold chain around her neck. "This means that I am married to the god," she would say confidently. But if her guardian heard her, she would demand that the child conceal the necklace again, for marriage to the god is something that they preferred to keep as secret as possible.

No wonder Amy cried out with tears day after day! But then, suddenly, after years of searching and waiting, the windows of heaven opened. Mr. and Mrs. Walker left India for a year, and they prayed with Amy that the Lord would increase the size of His flock. And the Lord gave Amy wisdom finally to discover and rescue several children.

One night Amy and Ponnammal hid in a barn where they could hear the conversation in the house next door through the thin walls. A man was going to sell his little daughter to a temple priest! By God's grace, the two Christian ladies were able to meet the man and talk him into giving them the little girl before the priest came back to get her.

Another father said he would give the missionaries his little girl in exchange for a hundred rupees.

"A hundred rupees?" Ponnammal cried. "We cannot buy the children! And for such a cost! Why, if we pay that amount for one child, no Indian will want to give us his child without a price."

"But perhaps we should pay it, Ponnammal," Amy suggested, "to rescue a soul."

"Amma," Ponnammal pleaded, "I hate to disagree with you—indeed, when have I ever disagreed with you?—but I know my people. They love money. There is a saying—'Say *money*—' "

' "And a corpse will open its mouth,' " Amy finished. "I know the saying. But I think that maybe the Lord would have us do it just this once. Let's pray fervently about it, to know the Lord's will in the matter."

After praying, Amy said, "This is what I think the Lord would have us to do, Ponnammal. We will buy the child, since it must be done at once. Then we will ask the Lord for one hundred rupees from a place that we did not expect it. That is a large amount, and if it comes in, we will know it is of the Lord."

They bought the child, even though Ponnammal was still doubtful. But just ten days after the little girl came to live with them, a fellow missionary sent Amy one hundred rupees—just the amount they needed! Amy gathered all the mission family together, and they sat in a circle and thanked God for His provision.

After that, Amy and Ponnammal tried to be always ready at a moment's notice to race to the rescue of a child that the temple women were about to snatch away, to try to convince the child's parents to give her to them instead.

Often the village that they needed to go to was many miles away. Word would come of a child in danger, and the missionaries at Dohnavur were always prepared. The pattern of their actions was almost always the same. Amy snatched up her traveling bag—"Not a moment to lose!"—and jumped into a bandy, urging the driver, "Go faster, faster! Oh, can't you go any faster?" The bandy lurched wrenchingly from side to side as the driver tried to oblige by snapping the reins against the backs of the lumbering oxen. Amy's stomach felt as if it were in her throat, but still the picture of the temple loomed before her eyes and she cried, "Faster, please, faster!" Finally the bandy dropped her off at a bus stop where Amy could no longer cry "faster, faster," and she waited for hours in the scorching heat for a bus to come by. One bus after another did chug past the corner, but each was already overflowing with passengers. Amy felt the heat beat against her head and tear at her limbs. "Please Lord," she prayed, "please help us to get there on time. And help me not to faint." Finally, after several hours, a ramshackle bus stopped to pick her up. Amy climbed on and found space where she could, shoving

herself between people and animals. She chafed at the maddening slowness of the driver, chafed every time he had to stop to let someone off or pick someone up.

The bus stopped. This was as close to her destination as Amy could get on this vehicle. That meant waiting for another bus or taking a bandy the rest of the way. Amy usually took a bandy rather than wait. She held her stomach and prayed, begging the driver to go faster.

That was the village! Now, which house could it be? There, she felt sure that was it. She stood outside and clapped until the door was answered. Then she would beg with the mother to reconsider and give the child to her.

Sometimes she was successful. Sometimes she was not. Sometimes she took this excruciating trip only to find that the temple women had already spirited the child away.

One Christian woman, named Old Devai, became as concerned as Amy for the children in danger. Because she was an elderly Indian woman, she was just right for this kind of work. She labored long and hard to get to the children before the temple women did, because the temple women were quick. Sometimes Old Devai would travel for more than a day to get a child that she had heard about, only to find that the temple women had gotten there only moments before and had stolen her away. But Old Devai never lost heart—she kept right on searching for the children, traveling many miles in her quest, sometimes getting little sleep. Often she was successful, and she brought many precious children to Dohnavur.

But sad things happened too. Some of the tiny babies died within just a few days or weeks of coming to the mission. "Old Devai traveled for days to bring this baby here," Arulai sobbed. "She pleaded with her mother until the Lord finally opened her heart to us. And now He has taken her. Why? Why?"

Amy's eyes were wet too, but she put her arm around Arulai's shoulders. "We mustn't think 'Why,' Arulai. I don't know the reason, but the Lord does. He can see through the blackness of our night here to see the light on the other side. He knows the reason each little one is taken. She is with Him."

One beautiful little girl, Lala, came to the compound when she was five years old. But she had been there only a month to hear about the goodness of Jesus when her family decided that they wanted her back. Nothing that Amy could do could keep them from taking her. With tears in her eyes Amy watched the bandy drive away. Then she trudged to her room and shut the door. "Lord," she prayed, "did that little girl understand anything we told her? She is so young! Please protect her soul."

The answer came back to her in a verse she had read, "Said I not unto thee, that, if thou wouldest believe, thou shouldest see the glory of God?" The Lord did protect Lala's soul. Just a month after she had gone home, she died. Word came back to Amy that as she died she had said, "I see three people in shining white. I am going to Jesus!"

Even though every death was a heartbreaking one to the Christians at Dohnavur, there were still many children to care for, and more were coming all the time in answer to Amy's prayers. By the end of two years she had seventy children! More helpers were needed, and the Lord provided those just as unfailingly as He had provided other needs. A trained nurse (for which they had been praying for some time) came to live at Dohnavur and help care for the sick children. And some of the Starry Cluster realized that they could serve the Lord just as well by staying at Dohnavur and caring for the children as they could by traveling and witnessing in villages.

It was around this time that the tradition of celebrating Coming Days was begun. Almost none of the children knew the date of their birth; so they instead celebrated the day that they had come to Dohnavur. The little honoree would dress up with a ribbon in her hair to be the center of attention for the whole day and receive a small bar of scented soap— a gift greatly prized by the beauty-loving Dohnavur children.

A great blessing came to Amy shortly after the first temple children started coming. Her mother, whom she hadn't seen for nine years, came to visit when the Walkers returned from England. She stayed almost two years. What a help she was in teaching Amy how to care for all those tiny children! And her mother's heart showed concern for her own daughter too. Amy had always had a tendency to work herself until she was sick and not think about her own needs at all. "This is all very good of you, dear," Mrs. Carmichael chided, "but you will certainly send yourself to an early grave if you don't eat properly and get the rest that you need. You are not a physically strong person, you know. You suffer from this neuralgia, and the Lord will not be honored by your ruining your own body."

"Oh, my darling mother," Amy laughed. "I've loved reading the letters that you sent so faithfully, but I certainly have missed your presence. I will try to take care of myself better. Somehow the Lord always gives me the strength to go on."

Chapter Twenty-one
Muttammal

"So children grow up good here at Dohnavur, do they?" Amy asked with a smile. Her heart was touched by the little twelve-year-old's words.

"Oh, yes, that is what I hear." Earnest little Muttammal took advantage of her mother's temporary absence from the room to lower her voice to a whisper and say, "Missie Carmichael, it is not just my uncle that I want to get away from. My mother and her sister are wicked women." She blushed at the thought of some unnamed horror. "If I cannot get away from them, I know I shall never grow up good."

"We will certainly do what we can, Muttammal," Amy promised.

Just then the little girl's mother reentered the room, waving her arms. "We must keep her away from her uncle, you see?" she stated emphatically. "He would marry her off to a man of his choosing. And then what would happen to the fields that her father left her when he died? They would all go to her uncle, I tell you. I must leave her here for safekeeping."

"I will be glad to take care of her," Amy responded warmly.

"Good." The woman seemed relieved. "I will come for her later." And she was gone.

"Oh, I am so glad to be here!" Muttammal's face shone. "Promise me that you will not let her take me away."

"But I cannot promise that, little one."

"But you said that your God answers prayer! Surely He would answer the prayer of a little girl."

"Indeed He does hear and answer the prayers of all those that love Him. We can teach you about Him while you are here."

"Will Jesus make me be good all the time?"

"He can give you the power to be good. And then you choose. No Hindu god can give you that kind of power."

Muttammal was beginning to understand more and more about the love of Jesus as Easter Sunday approached. But no one knew the awful scene that awaited them when it dawned.

"Give the child back to me!" It was Muttammal's mother at the door. "I am here to claim her. I have found someone that I want her to marry."

"Save me, save me from her, please!" Muttammal whispered, clinging to Amy's sari, hiding behind it the best she could.

"B-but, ma'am," Amy faltered, praying for wisdom, "we did not expect you today. Muttammal is not quite ready. Could you possibly return for her tomorrow?"

"Tomorrow?" The woman seemed to become angry, but then she relented. "Very well. I will continue to make preparations for the wedding. I will come back tomorrow."

For many hours Amy and Mr. Walker prayed for a miracle for the little Indian girl who was just beginning to learn about the love of Jesus.

But the Lord had mysterious plans for this child. He did not perform a miracle that night. The next morning Muttammal's mother was back, bringing with her several relatives. "Give the child to me!" she demanded. "I will not take any more of your excuses!"

This time Muttammal didn't bother to whisper. "Save me! Save me, Amma!" she cried.

But Amy could do nothing.

"Save you?" Muttammal's mother snorted. "I am here to save you from your uncle. You do not need to be saved from us!"

"Yes, come, you wicked child!" shouted Muttammal's aunt. "You must make preparations for your wedding."

"Please, please, Mr. Walker!" Muttammal ran to him and threw her arms around him. "Please do not let them take me away!"

But Mr. Walker could do nothing, because the little girl was too young. Muttammal's mother grabbed her and pulled her away, dragging her through the streets screaming. For many minutes Amy could still hear the shouts. "No! No! Save me, Amma Carmichael! Save me!"

"Oh, Lord," Amy sobbed, "sometimes it is so hard to hope in You."

But Amy continued to pray and tried to hope. The light shone for her when Muttammal's marriage didn't take place after all. Her mother granted permission for Amy to come visit and read to her from a Bible story book. But while Amy was there, Muttammal's uncle stormed into the room with some of his friends, angry and shouting. Amy had to leave. She prayed that nothing would happen to little Muttammal.

Then weeks went by. Amy prayed and prayed. She talked to lawyers and anyone else she could to find out how she could possibly get this little girl and keep her.

Both the uncle and the mother wanted Muttammal. Neither one of them trusted the other. Finally both of them agreed to give the child over to Amy while they settled their case. The little girl was saved and came to learn more and more about Jesus and to love Him dearly as her Saviour.

Once Muttammal's uncle tried to take her away, and once her mother came to seize her, but both times Amy went to court with a Christian lawyer, and the Lord preserved Muttammal in her care.

"You will not ever let them take me away, will you, Amma?" Muttammal insisted.

In an impulsive moment, Amy answered, "No, I won't, little one." Her heart felt cold, though. How could she ever keep a promise like that?

Once again the matter of who should have charge of Muttammal went to court. Amy stood in the courtroom listening as the judge made the decree that Muttammal should be given to her mother. But the words that should have given her a terrible feeling of despair somehow lifted her heart in a profound feeling of joy. She felt a joy that she had never felt before in all her life. "Somehow I know," she whispered to herself, "I just know that the Lord is going to work all this out."

When she got back home to Dohnavur, Amy found that Muttammal was gone. But it was too soon for her mother to have been able to come and get her. In fact, she found out that no one had seen her leave or seemed to have any idea where she was!

What had happened was that the previous night, shortly after the awful news had come back to the mission compound, a friend of Amy's named Mabel decided to help. She was just visiting and planning to leave that night anyway. So she sneaked into Muttammal's room where the little girl was sleeping.

"Get up, Muttammal!" she whispered. "You must run for your life."

"What?" Muttammal quickly rubbed the sleep out of her eyes. "Is my mother coming for me?"

"She will come soon if we don't hurry. Come to my room. Here. Put on this outfit."

"But these are a boy's clothes!"

"Of course. Not many people would think of looking for a little Hindu girl under the clothes of a Muslim boy. Now hurry!"

Muttammal quickly obeyed. Then Mabel showed her which way to go and sent her on her way with prayers.

A bandy was waiting for her outside the gate, and Muttammal was able to escape. She traveled from city to city, finally ending up in China, where she stayed for several years.

But Amy really wanted Muttammal back in India with her. Would it ever be possible? Amy spoke to a young man that she thought might be interested in marrying Muttammal, who was now a young woman. He wrote to her, and she wrote back. Soon they were engaged, and Muttammal was able to return to India. For many years Muttammal and her husband lived near the missionaries, helping them in their work and ministering for Christ. Jesus had indeed given Muttammal the power to "grow up good."

Chapter Twenty-two
Triumph in Tragedy

"Yes," Mr. Walker was saying, "and there's another one in northern India who works all by herself. A remarkable woman."

Amy shivered a little even though the night breeze was warm. She gazed up at the multitude of stars and said, "Well, the Lord knows what we can handle. I don't think I could ever bear the responsibility of this mission on my own shoulders. I'm so glad to have you and Mrs. Walker, even though she hasn't been able to do much in the last few years. I've really missed her since she had to go back to England. I certainly don't want to have to do all this myself."

Mr. Walker smiled. "You don't have to," he said. Amy sighed with joy and relief. Yes, the Lord knew that she needed someone to go to for advice and counsel.

"Even though it seems that you're not here very much at all!" she laughed. "And now leaving for another series of meetings. How long will you be gone this time?"

"No longer than you can handle on your own with the Lord's help, little sister," Mr. Walker returned. "I promise."

Just a few days after Mr. Walker had left for his meetings, another precious child went home to be with Jesus. Ponnammal was the worst hurt by this death, for Lulla had been her special favorite. But only six days after that, as Amy was still trying to comfort Ponnammal, two telegrams came. One was written two days earlier than the other, but somehow they had arrived at the same time. The first one told Amy that Mr. Walker was very sick. With a trembling hand she opened the second. All it said was "Revelation 22:4." Quickly she got her Bible and looked up the verse. The first part of the verse read, "And they shall see his face." Tears sprang to Amy's eyes as she thought of the true counselor and advisor she had lost. But then she thought of Mrs. Walker. "She hasn't even gotten to see her husband for some time," Amy thought. "And Ponnammal, poor Ponnammal, who is still mourning over the loss of little Lulla." She quickly went to Ponnammal to tell her the news and comfort her.

"But ah, Amma, this is a far worse blow to you than it is to me," the trusty Indian woman said. "You have lost your own big brother."

"Yes," Amy said, and she finally let herself cry a little.

"But still," Ponnammal continued, "do you remember what you said one night, that the Lord knew what you could handle yourself? He still knows. He will come to be even sweeter to you because He will be your strong arm now—He has made sure that you will have no other."

"Oh, Ponnammal, I am so thankful for you!" Amy cried.

Time passed, and the Lord provided more workers as they were needed to help with the great work that Amy was called to do. By 1913 the Dohnavur family numbered about one-hundred fifty. Little children ran everywhere, and there were always a number of babies howling and cooing in the nursery. One day as Amy was overseeing the construction of yet another new building for the mission, she looked around at the children and then saw Ponnammal and Arulai, now in her twenties, keeping a watchful eye on the little ones, along with some of the newer helpers. A memory came to her of a time not long before when a pastor visiting from back home had taken a tour of the grounds at Dohnavur. He had seen all the little houses where the workers and children lived, each worker having about a dozen little ones under her care. "How much do you pay these women?" he had asked, much impressed.

Amy had answered, "This work is expensive, for they have to be up at all hours of the day and night. In fact, it is too expensive to pay for; so none of us get any salary. We all do it through love."

As she remembered this, Amy prayed, "Lord, they have never asked for any pay. No pay! You answered the prayer of my heart of so many years ago to give me Indian Christians that count service for You more important than money. And You have provided all the money we need to build these wonderful buildings.

I praise You for all Your goodness to us. And how I thank You for Ponnammal and Arulai."

But only a few months later, in the spring of 1913, Ponnammal became ill. She found it hard to walk without pain. The nurse, Mabel Wade, was away; so Ponnammal had to be taken to a distant hospital. She had cancer.

The brave Indian woman endured two operations to remove cancer while Amy stayed with her, leaving Arulai in charge of the mission. But the doctor said to Amy, "Even now, after having done all I can do, I still can't be sure that the cancer won't return. I'm truly sorry."

Amy nodded and determined to trust the Lord for Ponnammal's full healing. After all, the Lord had taken Mr. Walker already. It was unthinkable that He would also take her most trusted Indian helper.

As she thought about these things, Amy received a letter from Arulai telling of a terrible malaria epidemic that had swept through the Dohnavur compound and left seventy children sick at once. But Arulai's spirits were still high. She told of the special strength and sweetness that the Lord gives in hard times.

Amy and Ponnammal were finally able to return to Dohnavur that summer. There Amy received a telegram stating that her mother had gone home to heaven. "My own dear mother," Amy whispered. "Our greatest prayer warrior in England. Lord, I know that to be with You is far better. But she was such a strong Christian, uplifting us before Your throne. And I did love her so dearly." She felt the tears coming again, fast and hard. "How I thank You that I shall see her again!"

Ponnammal had a third operation and seemed to get a little better. But as the months passed, she began to grow weak again and be in much pain. In 1914 it was discovered that her cancer had returned. For several months she had to stay in bed almost all the time.

"Why don't you pray the prayer of healing?" other people wrote to Amy, referring to James 5:14-15. "Ponnammal might be made well and returned to you to work many more years in India. Just take the Lord at His word."

But as sad as Amy was, she said, "I want the Lord's will to be done, not my own. I want Him to show Himself powerful in whatever way He chooses. If it is in raising Ponnammal up, I will praise His name. If it is in giving me the strength to carry on without her, I will praise His name." But Amy's heart still grieved over the thought of losing a friend so faithful.

During the days when the Starry Cluster had traveled to witness, Ponnammal had been Amy's favorite traveling companion and a bright testimony to the saving power of Jesus. And in later years, when the women had volunteered to stay at Dohnavur and care for the children, Ponnammal had adapted to that work as easily as if she had been doing it all along. Someone had once had to stay up at night when all of the children had fevers of 104 or more: Ponnammal. Someone had been needed to mix the medicine for those sick children, being careful to do it exactly right, for little lives lay in the balance: Ponammal. Someone had to be willing to follow divine instructions sometimes rather than following the instructions written on the bottles: Ponnammal. Someone had to travel to the distant marketplace to buy in quantity all the products that would keep for a long time— and be willing to haggle with the sellers for a good price and make sure that the rice wasn't full of worms or the rope rotted through: Ponnammal. Someone had to haggle with the milk seller when he came every morning and every evening to sell the milk that wouldn't keep more than a few hours without spoiling. Someone had to make sure that it wasn't tainted or watered down: Ponnammal. Someone had to hire the builders for the mission buildings and then make sure that they did their work and didn't try to run off with the money and some flimsy excuse. Once again it had been Ponnammal.

Amy watched in torment as Ponnammal suffered the unspeakable pain of cancer for weeks and months. There was no medicine for some time, but when the pain was worst, the Lord sent her heavenly music that helped her sleep. Then, in August of 1915, Amy's friend and helper for eighteen years saw the face of Jesus.

Although she was torn over this loss, Amy saw an opportunity to be a witness to the Hindu people around her.

"You know how Hindus act at a funeral," she began, looking at the many tear-stained faces as the Dohnavur family gathered around her. Everyone nodded. They had all seen Hindu funerals.

"The Hindus wail and cry at their funerals because they have no hope," Amy continued. "This is our chance to show them that Christians are different.

We do have hope—the wonderful hope of Jesus Christ Himself, that He has taken Ponnammal to heaven with Him. And she doesn't have cancer any more! No more pain! Christ has overcome death! And we have the precious hope that we will see her again."

The children smiled quavering little smiles. They all had loved Ponnammal dearly and all missed her sorely. But they knew that their Amma spoke the truth.

Ponnammal's funeral was a day to be remembered. Amy and the Dohnavur family gathered bright flowers of all different colors and arranged them in the room where Ponnammal's body lay. White flowers were laid around her body.

The village people came, quiet, waiting to see how Christians responded to the death of one that had been so loved and honored.

The Dohnavur family paraded through the streets to the burial site, not dressed in mourning garb, but dressed in their brightest colors, blues and whites and yellows. They were still sad, and some of them cried, but they did not wail uncontrollably as the Hindus did. Some of them even sang a song of rejoicing.

The Hindus watched in wonder. "I have never seen anything like it," said one man.

"We can show these people that death is not a complete loss," Amy said, "but only a farewell until we see each other again on the other side."

But back at the mission compound Amy felt a surge of grief again. Although she would see Ponnammal in heaven, she would never see her again here on earth, never hear her wise words of counsel, comfort, encouragement, and faith. "It is hard, so hard, my Father," she sobbed. "But Thou hast not left me comfortless. Thou art a strong arm to me. And I still have my faithful Arulai to help with the work."

But was the Lord going to take Arulai too? In December of that year, Arulai, who had been suffering from an illness, lay near death. Amy watched her and thought, "The Lord is going to knock out all the props from under me. The third one of my faithful three— He will take her too. My precious treasure, my Arulai." It was a hard day for Amy when she gave the word that a pastor be called to conduct one more funeral.

But even after the pastor had arrived and Arulai had come so close to heaven that she could see Mr. Walker and Ponnammal—even then the Lord gave her back. Arulai recovered miraculously and lived many more years.

All through the months that Ponnammal was dying, and as Arulai was sick, Amy still felt the terrible pain of neuralgia over and over. And as she thought of how long Ponnammal had lingered, she wrote in her diary, "Lord, grant this my earnest request. When my day's work is done, take me straight home. Do not let me be ill and a burden or anxiety to anyone. Thou knowest there could be no joy if I knew I were tiring those whom I love best, or taking them away from the children. Let me die of a battle wound, O my Lord, not of a lingering illness."

Chapter Twenty-three
The Forest

Just about every year since she had been in India, Amy had spent at least part of the two hot seasons, May and September, in a hill resort called Ootacamund. There she found a little relief from the neuralgia pains that plagued her, there she could be refreshed, and there she had time to write newsletters and poems and an occasional book. Often she took several other members of the Dohnavur family with her.

But after Mr. Walker had died, Amy didn't want to spend the hot days in Ootacamund any more. The main reason was that she thought it was too expensive.

"So we'll just have to look for a cool, refreshing place close to Dohnavur," she concluded.

"The only place you'll find anything like that is up in the mountains," Arulai observed. "And you know how steep they are around here. He who slips, dies."

"Well, it can't do any harm to look," Amy said. "As long as we're careful."

Amy did find a lovely spot in the mountains, and a cabin was already there that the Dohnavur family was allowed to use. For a couple of years she resorted there with some of the Dohnavur group, but the place was too small to hold very many of them.

"It is lovely, though," Amy said ruefully as she looked out at the other mountains, stretching over the horizon into infinity, it seemed.

"Amma, I saw another bear hole!" A child jumped up and down around Amy, interrupting her reverie.

"That's nothing. Amma, we saw some fresh *tiger* tracks. Come and see!" Two other children pulled on Amy's sari.

"Shh!" Amy put her finger to her lips and knelt down beside the three. "Look—do you see the others coming back from the river? Maybe they saw the tiger tracks too. Let's hide behind this tree and growl at them!"

The children's eyes danced, and they suppressed giggles as all four ran and hid.

Terrible growls issued from behind the shrubs as the unsuspecting women and girls walked up the path from the river. All of them shrieked and ran to the house. Then they came back out, afraid, but armed with sticks, creeping toward the source of the roars. When there was another terrible growl and a shaking of the bushes, some of the younger ones ran toward the sound. They were frightened, but they believed that their dear Amma was being eaten alive, and they were determined to rescue her.

Just then Amy and the three children walked out of the bushes as if nothing had happened. "Why, whatever is the matter?" asked Amy, brushing leaves from her skirt.

"Bear!" the others shouted. "In the bushes! Hurry!"

"But you are safe," one woman said, breathless with relief. "Thanks be—"

Then a giggle escaped from a little girl behind Amy. "It was a trick!" the woman cried, shaking her stick at the guilty ones. "You scared us so . . ."

"Oh, Amma, you tricked us!" all the children gathered around the woman that they loved and pulled her back into the house where she could tease them for being so frightened.

Amy loved to play with the children, thinking up tricks to play with—and on—them. She knew how important it was for the little ones to forget the lives they had left behind and be happy in the new lives they had found. But even as she joked and teased with them on the outside, she still cried out on the inside for the thousands of other children who still needed to be rescued.

When Amy returned to Dohnavur after that trip, she knew that she had to find another place of refreshment, a place that would be big enough and that they would be able to call their own. She and some friends began to go hiking in the forest mountains, hour after hour, day after day, looking for just the right spot. She determined not to become discouraged, even though the search was beginning to look hopeless.

Then someone told them about the Grey Jungle, a special place hidden high in the forest mountains. And as soon as Amy saw it, she knew it was the place the Lord wanted for the Dohnavur family. A river, waterfalls, pools, beautiful trees for shade, and lush grass—all of it was here, a perfect place to stay cool in the hot months and return to the work renewed and refreshed.

The Lord provided the money for the Grey Jungle, and they bought it in 1917, when Amy was forty-nine years old. Then they began to build.

But getting the buildings built proved to be a more difficult matter than Amy had bargained for.

"Can't you work any faster?" Amy asked the carpenter and the masons somewhat impatiently. "Do you have to take three naps a day?"

The carpenter shrugged lazily. "You want things so much faster than they can be done," he drawled. "It is no wonder that you are called the *Musal Ammal*. You jump from here to there to do things so fast. Taking several naps every day—it is our custom."

"Well, our custom," Amy countered, "is to get the roof on a building before the rainy season sets in. Will you be able to do it?"

"Certainly." One of the masons eyed her with a calculating glance. "If we have enough money."

Amy sighed.

Later she talked with some of the workers and children. "You remember, Amma," Arulai said, "that to an Indian, work is something to be avoided if at all possible. The only incentive for the average Indian to work is to get money."

"How well I know," Amy sighed despondently. "But what can we do? The rainy season is almost upon us, and the roof isn't on the Forest House yet. The walls are barely even built."

"We can pray for wisdom in dealing with these men," Arulai suggested.

"Yes, and for patience," Amy added ruefully.

When several of them had prayed, one of the children spoke up. "Amma, we are not afraid to work. We will do what the workmen should be doing!"

"You?" Amy asked doubtfully. "But you don't know how—"

"We know how to carry bricks and tiles."

"And gather buckets of mud. Do let us help, Amma! We'll show the workmen that we can do as well as they. Better, even."

"We'll show them that Christians know how to work! Please let us!"

And so it happened that the sleepy-eyed workmen watched in wonder as children marched past them with the mud, bricks, and tiles that they themselves should have been carrying. They heard the children singing a song that Amy had written. "Hate not laborious work! Joy, joy is in it."

"What is that song those children sing?" an amused workman asked. "Where do they learn such ideas?"

Amy felt particularly feisty. "It is a song you would do well to learn yourself," she replied.

Finally the men felt a little guilty and got the house finished. But not before the rainy season had come and the walls had caved in—twice—just as Amy had feared.

Partly because of the testimony of the children, two workmen accepted Christ before the building was finished. They were the first people to be baptized in the beautiful pool on the property.

Amy loved the Forest, as she called it, as she had loved few places. There she could rest and write. Some of the poems she wrote were silly ones just for the children, and they loved to hear her recite them. "Amma, do 'The Elephant' again, please!" the little ones would beg. And as Amy put on her most serious poetry-reciting face, they would lean over and make their arms into trunks to imitate the wild elephants they had seen.

The elephant comes with a tramp, tramp, tramp,
The elephant comes with a stamp, stamp, stamp,
  Through forest and over marshy ground
  His great big flat feet pound and pound
  With a rumpety—dumpety—crumpety sound.

See, here's a tangle of maidenhair,
Among the pandanus spikes down there;
  And right through the very middle of it
  He's trampled exactly as he saw fit
  With his blundery—wondery—dundery wit.

A fool, do you think? No, he's no fool,
Look at the track, it leads to a pool,
  And on and on to a shady place
  Where he can fan his beautiful face
  With a jungelly—tumbelly—scrumbelly grace.

Chapter Twenty-four
Answers to Prayer

One day Amy stood by a waterfall all alone, watching the rushing water come pouring over the cliff. She was thinking about a matter that had come back to her time and again for some years now.

Boys. Little boys. She knew that the Dohnavur mission was only for girls, but she hadn't been able to get boys out of her mind since she had known that they sometimes went into temple service too. Even more of them were wanted by drama companies. They were on the lookout for any bright, handsome young Indian boy, ready to promise him a life of riches and fame. But Amy knew that a boy who grew up living in a drama company would not grow up good, and would most likely have no opportunity to hear about the Lord Jesus.

For several years now these thoughts had come back to her. Mr. Walker had told her that she had enough to do with the girls' work, and she knew that she did. Taking care of boys would mean building a whole new set of buildings, getting a whole new set of workers. . . . "But would You provide that,

Lord? If it is Your will for these little ones to be rescued, then surely You would."

And the Lord answered this prayer too. One little boy came to the mission before anyone outside the compound even knew that Amy wanted to take boys. Somehow, through the grace of God, provision was made for him and others until buildings could be built.

They had to pray for the provision of their daily needs as well. But they also worked diligently, because, as Amy reminded them, " 'It is required in stewards, that a man be found faithful.' "

Every year the members of the Dohnavur family planted their own rice crop. They counted on this to feed them for the coming year, just as villagers counted on their own rice crops to do the same. But one year the weather grew unexpectedly hot when it should have been cold. The caterpillars in their cocoons thought it was summertime, thought they were butterflies by now, and hatched. But they were still caterpillars! So they promptly began to eat the rice seedlings, both in Dohnavur and in the surrounding villages. The crops for the entire next year would be lost! While the Hindus beseeched their idols and offered sacrifices to them, the members of the Dohnavur family began to pray. "Lord, please save the rice crops," they prayed. "Ours and the villagers' too, if it please You."

This time it pleased the Lord to save only the crops of Dohnavur. Two days later a child looked out the window. "Come and see! Come and see!" she cried. There were hundreds of big white birds devouring the caterpillars. "He answered our prayers!"

People in England began to learn more about Amy's work with children from the many books she wrote, often describing the antics of the little girls she cared for—who were not always little angels. Many children in Britain learned to love these girls that they had never met and wanted to send their few pennies to the work of Dohnavur. Around Christmas time one year, a box of toys arrived for the children, along with a note from the mother of an eight-year-old boy from Ireland. "Robin read about your work and saved his money all year to buy your children a box full of Christmas toys. He sent them off with joy some weeks ago, but the ship that carried them sank. I then offered to let him buy more—with the money that I was going to use to buy his own Christmas presents. He thought it over quite soberly for a while, but the Lord must have impressed something on his heart, for when he came back to me, his face was shining. He said, 'Mother, I want to do it! Let's hurry and go shopping again!' "

But some people back in England complained. "Is this really mission work you are doing?" they said. "Just taking care of children and raising crops and building buildings? You aren't out winning souls!"

"Well," Amy observed, "you cannot save and then pitchfork souls into heaven! And as for buildings, souls (in India, at least) are more or less securely fastened into bodies. Bodies cannot be left to lie about in the open, and as you cannot get the soul out and deal with it separately, you have to take them both together."

Amy was indeed concerned about the bodies that her little girls and boys and her adult workers had to live in. Sometimes they, like her, were sick or injured. She longed for a hospital and a doctor to help them physically so that they could serve the Lord more perfectly. She thought about a hospital and prayed for the Lord to heal the sick for many months.

Then she heard about another place where Christians had seen the Lord heal many of the sick among them. They gave God all the glory for it. Amy was encouraged by the news. One reason for her gladness was that India, sunk so deep in idol worship, was like a place spiritually under lock and key. Many Christians despaired of ever being able to see the power of God in that desolate place. Another reason was that she and the others were weary of seeing so many people desperately ill. Amy prayed with renewed faith for the Lord to heal the many sick children and town people who came to the English missionaries seeking help. The very next morning one of the workers, who was in pain, came to her, crying, "Lay hands on me, Amma!"

"But I don't have the power to heal," Amy objected. "All the power is in Jesus Christ."

But the worker put Amy's hands on the place of her pain and asked Amy to pray for healing. "But there is no power in my hands to heal!" Amy objected. Yet she could not turn away a plea for her prayers. To Amy's surprise, the Lord did relieve the worker's pain. She was even able to complete her day's work.

Then a gardener came. He too asked for Amy to "lay hands on him." Though overwhelmed by the last experience, Amy still objected to anybody finding a power in her hands to heal, even if the apostles had done it. But she did pray for the man. The gardener was made well also, and he was able to go back to his labor, glorifying and praising God.

Amy thought that perhaps the Lord was answering prayers in this unusual way in order to help establish His Word in India, where so many people did not know about Him. As sick children in the compound were brought forward in the prayer meetings, all of the Dohnavur family prayed for the Lord to continue healing their bodies. And many of the children were healed—some by the next day, others within a few hours.

People from the villages heard about these miracles. They also brought their sick for the Christians at Dohnavur to pray for. But, as might have been expected, many of these superstitious people attributed the healing to Amy. She was concerned over the many exaggerations and rumors that were spreading about the prayer meetings at Dohnavur.

Also, other Christians not as well taught in Scripture wrote to Amy and to other missionaries to say that these miracles were the same as the early church's gifts of healings. They suggested that Amy pray for the type of outpouring of the Holy Spirit as was seen in the Acts of the Apostles.

Amy, for a time confused over all this advice, prayed for the Lord's guidance in these matters. She felt certain that He wanted a hospital built at Dohnavur. After all, though many of the children had been healed by God through the power of prayer, He had also given her definite direction to take some to distant hospitals where they would be healed through medical treatment. And others He had not healed but rather had taken them home to heaven.

So Amy prayed for His wisdom in knowing *how* to pray.

Amy knew that some of the people were being healed. But she knew that the power to heal came from God, and not from her. And she also knew that she could not command God to heal; though she prayed with consistent faith, God did not always choose to heal the one for whom she prayed. Sometimes God chose to take the sick person home to Himself; sometimes God allowed the person to remain sick, for in sickness God often helps His children grow. Amy knew that all she could do was to cast her burden upon the Lord and to accept as His will whatever He sent.

Not long after, the unusual cases of healing ceased. The villagers, no longer seeing what they were coming to regard as a show, lost interest in the mission. But the prayer meetings at Dohnavur continued. There was still guidance needed and the faith to continue God's work in a dark land and the daily cleansing from sin.

But Amy still saw the sick all around her, and she knew that it was time to pray in earnest for a hospital and to begin making plans.

Chapter Twenty-five
Amy Meets Robin Hood

"You mean he actually does rob from the rich and give to the poor?" Amy could hardly believe her ears.

"Yes, Missie," the man insisted. "All the poor people love him."

"Well, I should think so," Amy agreed. "It's amazing—a modern-day Robin Hood—and here in India!"

Amy was on her way down the mountain from the Forest, and the men carrying her chair loved telling her about the outlaw that everyone was talking about these days—Jambulingam.

"They say that he can leap over wells that are twenty feet across!" one man said.

"And he can escape from any prison ever built," said another.

"He takes what he needs, and if he takes it from a poor person, he makes sure that payment is made."

"He likes to call himself the Red Tiger," said another.

"I surely do wish I could meet Jambulingam and tell him about Jesus," Amy whispered to herself.

Only a few days later Amy's wish came true. She didn't know it, but Jambulingam and his men had been watching her and wanted to meet her. Then, one time when she was all alone, they leaped out before her.

"Greetings, missionary woman." The outlaw salaamed. "I am the one they call the Red Tiger."

Amy was a little surprised, but she kept her poise. "I have been looking forward to meeting you," she said. "I hear that you are wanted by police all over this area."

"Yes, I am," he answered. "But you must understand—the Indian police are corrupt. They do justice only when it serves their purpose. Would you like to hear my story?"

"I would love to," Amy answered eagerly.

"I was accused of a crime I did not commit. Because the police are more interested in bribes than in truth, I fled. Then I found that an enemy was telling lies about me. I grew even more afraid, and I ran to the mountains. I fear that I could never receive justice; so I stay here. But now my wife has died and there is no one to care for my three little children!"

Again Amy remembered the first Robin Hood, who also, according to tradition, was unjustly accused and fled to live in the forests of England.

"I have a request, missionary lady. Will you take care of my little ones?"

"I will be glad to help if you in turn will promise me one thing."

"If I can, I will."

"Never use your gun."

"Ah, I cannot promise that. I will promise never to use it except to protect my life. Otherwise I will have no defense."

"All right. Use your gun only in defense of your life."

"It is a bargain." Jambulingam smiled, showing a row of white teeth. "I like you, missionary lady!"

"I like you too, Robin Hood. I beg of you to surrender to the police."

"But the Indian police are corrupt, as I have said," the outlaw explained patiently. "If it will serve their purpose best, they will find me guilty of all kinds of things that I have never done."

"But what if you surrender to a British officer?" Amy urged. "He would be much more likely to be honest. Please forsake this life of stealing."

"I do like you, missionary lady." Jambulingam shook his head. "But I am still afraid of wicked police."

"But the Lord could protect you."

"Which Lord are you talking about?"

"Jesus Lord. The God of the universe—the one true God." And Amy seized the opportunity to explain to the outlaw a little bit about the God who had become man.

"This is very interesting—very new," Jambulingam said slowly. "Will you pray for me?"

"Let us pray together right now," answered Amy. And they knelt down.

For days as Amy went about her endless work, the thought of this Indian Robin Hood never left her mind for long. Over and over again she prayed, "Lord, let him come to truly know You. Give him the courage to surrender to the authorities. And please, Lord, don't let him be punished for anything he hasn't done."

But then word came to Amy that he and Kasi, a friend of his, had been trapped by the Indian police and put into jail. Amy prayed and was able to go in to see him and talk to him more about the Lord. "Please, Lord," she prayed, "please help him to know You."

Two months later, when Amy visited Jambulingam in jail, she found that he had given his life to the Lord and wanted to be baptized as proof of it. A visiting missionary baptized him.

Then for many months Amy was not allowed to visit Jambulingam. The only person allowed to see him was one Indian Christian. The Red Tiger's trial came, and he pleaded guilty to his robberies in the mountains but innocent to all the false charges. Still the trial went on. Then one day the visiting Indian Christian man read from Acts 12—the story of Peter's escape from prison.

"So the Lord helped this man out of his bonds, did He?" the outlaw mused. "Surely He can help another child of His to escape his fetters!" And the very next week Jambulingam and his friend, Kasi, escaped from prison. "The Lord has done it!" Jambulingam exclaimed. "Praise His name!"

But Amy was distraught. She knew that for Jambulingam to escape and become an outlaw again would mean only more troubles for him and a poor testimony for the Lord. "I didn't pray for him as I should have!" she chided herself. "He was such a very young Christian—it's my fault!"

Some of Amy's friends were able to get in touch with the two outlaws. "No, I will not go back to robbery," Jambulingam promised. "I have a new life now."

But Jambulingam's troubles were by no means over. Other robbers heard that the Red Tiger had escaped, and they began to use his name when they robbed. Now the cry, "We are Jambulingam and Kasi!" could be heard all over the territory, often in several different places on the same night.

Amy went to the police. "Please understand," she begged. "These men are not really responsible for any of the robberies taking place in their names."

"And how do you know that, missionary woman?" was the surly reply. "If you have such close contact with them, you should tell us where they are instead of trying to defend them!"

Amy went back home in despair. Still she tried to persuade the two outlaws to give themselves up to the British police. But they were afraid for their lives.

At last Amy was able to see the Red Tiger late one night in the middle of the forest. Jambulingam held her hands reverently as if she were his mother. "I have not robbed," he promised. But he went on to admit, "I have often been tempted to. After all, they think we are doing it. Why shouldn't we?"

"Don't despair, Robin Hood," Amy encouraged him. "Trust God to protect you and give yourself up."

"I cannot. I simply cannot." Jambulingam hung his head in despair. "I know now how wrong it was to escape from prison, but now I am too afraid to give myself up. They will kill me one day."

"If only you would die without a weapon in your hand," Amy begged. "Please remember your promise. This time don't kill even to protect your own life."

But Amy could not persuade him to give himself up. They prayed together and recited some Scripture, and she left with a prayer in her heart. Two months later, Amy heard that the men had been cornered and killed.

"But how did he die?" she begged the one who told her. "Did he die nobly? Did he have a weapon in his hand?"

"He was running up the hill with his gun. And they say that then he looked as if he remembered something. He turned, dropped his gun, and raised his hands toward heaven. They got him easily."

"It is enough," Amy sighed. "I will see him again. I know I will see him again."

Chapter Twenty-six
The Ministry at Dohnavur

The mission work at Dohnavur was growing and growing. Finally, in 1925, Amy and her faithful helpers thought that it would be a good idea to give their group a name. They decided to call themselves the Dohnavur Fellowship. People all over Europe, especially in England, wanted to be members of the Dohnavur Fellowship too, because they already prayed for Amy and her work. The headquarters of the Fellowship was always right there in Dohnavur, but a branch was started in London too.

Amy tried to treat every new member of the Fellowship as a new member of a family. But sometimes new missionaries came to work with her, labored enthusiastically for a while, and then left for the wrong reason. Sometimes they found the work dull—not at all the exciting and romantic missionary life they had imagined. Sometimes they decided that the heat was more than they could bear. And sometimes they grew discouraged with the hardness of the Hindus' hearts, and they sailed for home again.

Amy always wanted to blame herself when this happened. "Lord, maybe I didn't pray for that new missionary enough. Maybe I wasn't the example I should have been. Maybe I didn't spend enough time with him." Even though she was growing older and was often in pain, Amy tried harder and harder to at least see each person, and to speak with those who were having trouble . . . or causing trouble.

But in 1925 a special young man stopped by Dohnavur on his way to China, where he felt God had called him to be a missionary. His name was Godfrey Webb-Peploe.

"What a fine young man he seems to be," Amy thought to herself. "He gets along with the little boys so well—and we do so need the right man to lead these little boys. . . . But I mustn't think about that. God has called him to China."

Godfrey went on to China, but a year later his older brother Murray visited. He was on his way to China, too, to be a doctor there. Once again that longing was awakened in Amy, not only for a leader for the boys, but for a doctor in the hospital and for a leader for the Dohnavur Fellowship after she went to heaven. Even after Murray left, for days the thought kept coming back to her mind.

"But Lord," she said, "I know You want them for China. That country is every bit as needy as India, I'm sure. Please quiet my heart. I keep wanting them here so badly! They both seem to be just perfect for this work. I don't understand why You even sent them here when it's so clear that You want them somewhere else—it just showed me what it is we need so desperately. Oh, please forgive me for these thoughts."

After she was positive the Lord wanted her to, Amy went ahead and paid for the building of a compound for the boys. There was still no leader, but Godfrey and Murray kept coming back to her mind. Then, she received a telegram saying that Godfrey would like to come to visit! He was sick, and India had the kind of climate he needed to recover properly. Amy's heart jumped, but she prayed again, "Please quiet my heart. You need them for China."

But while he was visiting, she kept having the feeling that he and his brother would be perfect for carrying on the work at Dohnavur. Then, one morning, Amy woke up suddenly as though the Lord had spoken to her. A question burned in her mind. "Why have you never asked Me for Godfrey and Murray to help you with this work?" Amy was quiet for a moment, troubled. "Lord, You know why," she prayed. But the Lord seemed to say, "Ask Me now."

Amy was still troubled, but she rose and prayed. Finally she thought, "Well, I guess the Lord can take care of China too. He can use someone else there just as easily as He can use Godfrey and Murray here." But still she was doubtful.

On December 14th of that year, 1925, Godfrey talked about how he would soon be well enough to go back to China. And he even said to Amy, as if he knew her thoughts, "Don't count on me for anything here." Amy's heart fell.

But the very next day he wrote her a note and slipped it into her hand. "I don't feel worthy to join the Dohnavur Fellowship," he wrote, "but I know the Lord has called me here." Amy's heart sang. The next day, her fifty-ninth birthday, was a very happy one for her.

Some months later Murray too had to leave China because of a civil war. Dohnavur seemed like a likely place to go, because it was close and his brother was there. Murray intended to visit for just a few months, but after some time he realized that the Lord had called him to this work too. He asked Amy if he could stay on with her.

"Lord," Amy prayed as she rejoiced, "help me never to doubt Your word to me again."

Amy had been faithful in praying for the hospital that she had asked for years before. Now that Murray was with her, she felt sure that the Lord wanted her to start work on it. A godly Christian woman doctor, May Powell, had also come to work in Dohnavur, and the Lord seemed to say "Now."

They all decided that "Place of Heavenly Healing" would be the best name for a hospital that would be designed to glorify the Lord Jesus. Everyone was excited as plans began.

"We want to be sure to have a prayer room," Amy said. "That will be the very heart of the whole hospital. And we can ring the bells in the tower when special prayer is requested for an urgent need."

A beautiful but simple and practical building was planned, and the cost was figured. They found that it would cost ten thousand pounds in British money.

"Ten thousand pounds! That's so much," Murray exclaimed, a little breathless at the thought. "That's a terrible lot of money."

Amy was a little afraid to say anything. She didn't want to show a lack of faith to the workers gathered around her. But it really did seem like a huge sum of money.

"Let's all pray about it separately for several weeks," she finally said.

At last all the adult members of the Family met again and spent even more time in prayer together. Then Amy read I John 5:14 and 15. "And this is the confidence that we have in him, that, if we ask any thing according to his will, he heareth us: and if we know that he hear us, whatsoever we ask, we know that we have the petitions that we desired of him."

Then she solemnly wrote "Asked for, and received, according to I John 5:14, 15, ten thousand pounds for the Place of Heavenly Healing." Each worker signed his name. They were all ready to take their Lord at His word.

And the money did begin to come in. Just bit by bit, in very small amounts. Even the children, who loved their Amma and wanted to help in any way they could, collected fruit to sell and gave their coins to the hospital fund.

Some of the workers, though, were a little discouraged. "Maybe we should do without a maternity ward," they said. "We could put the women who are going to have babies someplace else in the hospital." But Dr. Powell and Dr. Webb-Peploe, as well as Amy, objected. They wanted to plan for this hospital with all the departments that the ten thousand pounds included, and that meant the maternity ward too.

Then one day a girl came running into the house in the middle of a Coming Day party. "A telegram! A telegram!"

With thumping heart—you could never tell if a telegram might mean someone had died—Amy took it and opened it. Her hand shook as she read, "One thousand pounds for maternity ward."

"A thousand pounds!" she exclaimed. "A thousand pounds! Why, that could build five maternity wards! That's a tenth of all the money we need! Oh, praise the Lord. Praise the Lord!"

Later she found how that money had come. A Christian man, while praying, had been led to pray for a gift of a thousand pounds to give to the Dohnavur mission. He was not rich, but "the Lord sent it out of the blue," he said. "Out of the blue," Amy thought. "The Lord sends a lot of His blessings from there. Sometimes they're just impossible to explain."

The hospital took several years to complete. As she stood watching the progress one day, Amy thought, "Lord, wouldn't it be wonderful if someday every single worker in this hospital could be one of the boys or girls You brought here to Dohnavur? If all who choose to could be trained to be doctors, nurses, orderlies, why, they would have a greater ministry here than they could have out in their villages, I do believe! People who come in to a hospital to be made well are usually so much more ready to hear about You than people who are already physically strong. These boys and girls could be Your evangelists while they stay right here in the mission compound! Oh, did I ever even imagine such a glory when I first came here! Truly, truly, You are a great God!"

A man who was visiting caught sight of Amy. "All these buildings," he said to a worker, waving his hands

in front of him, "all these buildings and you say that your ministry owes no money to anyone?"

"That is true, sir," the worker replied.

"How can that be? How is that possible?"

The worker was also watching Amy, whose tear-stained face gazed into heaven. The worker paused before answering. "It is only one of many 'impossible' things that have become possible," she replied slowly. "It is possible because of great faith. The great faith of a woman who believes a great God."

Epilogue

Many years before, Amy had prayed, "Lord, please don't let me linger when it's time for me to go. Please just take me." But in September of 1931 she prayed, "Do *anything,* Lord, that would fit me to serve Thee and help my beloveds."

The Lord saw fit to deny the first request while granting the second. The very month she had prayed her prayer of surrender, when Amy was sixty-three, she fell and had to be confined to bed. She wasn't able to walk again for almost twenty years, until she went home to heaven in 1951.

Even with all her pain, Amy had been very active around the mission compound before her fall, overseeing work here, speaking to a troubled worker there, playing with children over there. It was hard for her to be confined to bed, very hard. But the Lord had His purpose in even this, and while she was in bed, Amy was able to write over a dozen books, including the story of Arulai. Time had always been precious to her, and now she used that valuable time to pray for the ministry in Dohnavur. Amy had become used to spending hours at a time in prayer, fellowshiping with the Lord and interceding for others. During the last twenty years of her life, it was not unusual for her to spend an entire day with the Lord when there was a great need for prayer.

And, despite the fact that she could hardly ever leave her room, Amy continued to help administer the Dohnavur Fellowship. Children were permitted to visit her as her strength could bear it, and she continued to keep in touch with the workers.

Arulai was the one that Amy was counting on to take over the work with the girls when she died. In addition, she planned for Dr. Powell to take the hospital, and Godfrey and Murray the work with the boys. Amy truly did think that the Lord had these four all prepared to oversee this mission, and she felt content and ready to go.

But neither Arulai nor Godfrey had ever been very strong, and both of them died before Amy did. Then Murray had to return to England for family reasons. Only Dr. Powell was left. Once again Amy had to lean totally on the Lord rather than on her own understanding. And before she died she was able to see Him raise up other capable Christians to lead the other parts of the Dohnavur work.

For years Amy and the rest of the Dohnavur Family prayed for her healing. Finally she understood that it was not to be. Then she prayed that the Lord might take her home right away. She did so hate to be a burden to others! Although the Lord wouldn't promise her that, He did give her a promise that she would go without tearful good-byes— "I will take you in your sleep."

And so it was. On January 18, 1951, Amy Carmichael passed from sleep into the presence of the Lord Jesus.

Though there were many tears, the Dohnavur family tried to hold Amy's funeral in the very style that she had established as tradition so many years before at Ponnammal's death. The children covered her room with flowers, and the boys sang as the people streamed into the church to look one last time on the body that their beloved Amma had left behind— dressed in a sari, as they were so used to seeing her. Almost all of Amy's "children" were there—some of them mature women now. One of the men read Matthew 25:21, "Well done, thou good and faithful servant: thou hast been faithful over a few things, I will make thee ruler over many things: enter thou into the joy of thy lord."

And all of Amy's children, whom the Lord through her had rescued from a life of sin and shame, sang together.

"Alleluia! The strife is o'er, the battle won."